JOSEPH PEARCE is the author of *The Unmasking of Oscar Wilde, Solzhenitsyn: A Soul in Exile, Tolkien: Man and Myth, Literary Converts, Wisdom and Innocence: A Life of G.K. Chesterton* and *Bloomsbury and Beyond: The Friends and Enemies of Roy Campbell.* He is currently Writer in Residence at Ave Maria College in Ypsilanti, Michigan.

SMALL IS STILL BEAUTIFUL

Joseph Pearce

HarperCollins*Publishers*

For Susannah

HarperCollins*Publishers*
77–85 Fulham Palace Road,
Hammersmith, London W6 8JB

www.**fire**and**water**.com

This paperback edition 2002
1 3 5 7 9 8 6 4 2

First published in Great Britain by
HarperCollins*Publishers* 2001

Copyright © Joseph Pearce 2001

Joseph Pearce asserts the moral right to
be identified as the author of this work

A catalogue for this book is
available from the British Library

ISBN 0 00 714215 3

Set in Minion and Rotis Semi Sans

Printed and bound in Great Britain by
Clays Ltd, St Ives plc

Contents

Acknowledgements

This volume would scarcely have been possible without the generous help and cumulative effort of a host of individuals from a wide variety of organizations. These are listed, in no particular order, and I should like to apologize for any sins of omission.

Thanks to Richard Douthwaite, author of *The Growth Illusion*, who was kind enough to read through chapter two, 'Malignant Growth', and offered many valuable observations as well as suggesting a number of amendments, and to Alan Gear, Chief Executive of the Henry Doubleday Research Association (HDRA), who has expended much of his limited time in supplying material for the chapters on agriculture. Janet Bearman of Norfolk Organic Farmers has helped immensely in supplying source material and lists of helpful addresses, and Paul Wilkinson of Ecotech has been tireless and uncomplaining whenever his assistance has been requested. Thanks to Murree Groom of Crop Enhancement Systems for sharing his scientific expertise, and to Godric Bader, Andrew Gunn, Denise Sayer and Stuart Reeves of the Scott Bader Commonwealth who provided so much material for the chapters on co-operative ownership. Others who have helped in the research on co-operatives include Bob Allan of the Industrial Common Ownership Movement (ICOM), G. Turner of Equity Shoes, Mervyn G. Wilson of the Co-operative College in Loughborough, Gillian F. Lonergan of the Co-operative Union Ltd, David Dickman, Chief Executive of the UK Co-operative Council, Susan Jenkins of Triodos Bank and last but not least, Tonia Mihill, Ian Carey, Darren Slowther, Jane Taylor, Clare Bufton and Joel Rodker of the Treehouse Restaurant in Norwich. Thanks to them all.

Grateful acknowledgement is also due to the following people and organizations: David Hands of the Federation of Small Businesses, Ian Lowe of the Campaign for Real Ale, Maggie Brown of the Henry Doubleday Research Association, Lara Chamberlain (Soil Association), Jonathan Matthews (Norfolk Genetic Information Network), Susan Bayliss (Asda customer relations), Shirley Kidd (Tesco Customer Services Manager), Jacinta MacDermot (Centre for Alternative Technology), Fergal Martin (Catholic Truth Society), Stratford Caldecott (Centre for Faith and Culture) and Richard Adams (Contraflow). Material was also supplied by anonymous individuals from Greenpeace, Oxfam, the National Federation of City Farms and the Pesticides Trust. Individuals who have helped in various ways include Satish Kumar, Alfred Simmonds, Christopher Hughes, Russell Sparkes and Aidan Mackey.

James Catford, Amy Boucher Pye, Kathy Dyke, Heather Worthy and many others at HarperCollins have worked diligently to bring my labours to fruition, and I am particularly grateful to Sarah Hollingsworth for carefully reading each chapter and for her many observations and suggestions.

I would like to thank Catherine Trippett, Permissions Manager for Random House, for permission to quote extensively from E.F. Schumacher's *Small Is Beautiful*. The extract from *Sollicitudo Rei Socialis* by Pope John Paul II is published with the kind permission of the Catholic Truth Society, London.

The penultimate word of thanks must belong to Barbara Wood, E.F. Schumacher's daughter, who has been of invaluable help. Throughout the writing of this book she has been tireless in her advice, criticism and encouragement. Without her detailed appraisal of each chapter I have no doubt that this volume would have been greatly impoverished. I hope she will accept the following as a testament to her labour. Ultimately, however, the author must acknowledge the priceless contribution of Mrs Wood's late father. Without *Small Is Beautiful*, E.F. Schumacher's ground-breaking work, this endeavour would have been completely impossible. The following pages are intended both as a clarion cry, calling people to rally to the perennial wisdom of Schumacher's words, and a tribute to the spirit of the man himself.

Foreword

My father, E.F. Schumacher, had a very positive view of humankind. He believed that human beings were created in the image of God and should be defined by their greatest achievements rather than by average behaviour or by activities that were less than human. He was appalled when men and women were described in such terms as 'naked apes' which he thought could only lead to corresponding behaviour. 'Nothing is more conducive to the brutalization of the modern world than the launching, in the name of science, of wrongful and degrading definitions of man.'[1]

As an economist Schumacher recognized that such 'brutalization' had crept into economic thinking and in *Small Is Beautiful* he examined the consequences of this faulty anthropology. Human beings, bestowed with wonderful and creative gifts, with the potential for unimagined greatness, had become mere 'factors of production' to be eliminated where possible because of cost, efficiency or convenience. Capable of great and noble deeds and emotions, they were treated as though there was no greater happiness than that of ever increasing consumption. Although his book was about economics he did not believe that the problems he was analysing were essentially economic. The real problem, he maintained, was a moral one.

Schumacher was a practical man. He never moralized or spoke in abstract terms. Everything he said was rooted in real life and practical experience. This made his words powerful and memorable. He spoke to the deep longings inside ordinary people: to their longing for fulfilling creative work, to their search for meaning, to their desire for peace, beauty and permanence in a world of uncertainty and change. He spoke in the context of everyday human life and activity: the work place, the market place, and the living environment. He knew that if the human spirit – that part of ourselves that yearns for the infinite – was neglected then despair would set in. Spirituality must become part and parcel of our daily human existence once more, shaping it and giving it meaning.

His belief in the divine creation of humankind gave him faith in the power of ordinary people to change the world. His analysis of the modern world was a rallying call to action. He did not merely demand that 'something ought to be done' as so many other writers on similar issues did, shifting responsibility onto politicians, economists or scientists. Rather, he said that these matters were too important to be left to the experts. He put his hope in the fact that 'ordinary people are often able to take a wider view, and a more "humanistic" view, than is normally being taken by experts'.[2] He believed that ordinary people, who so often feel that they are utterly powerless, can discover their power not so much by acting on their own in setting up new initiatives, but when they give their sympathy and support to already existing groups of activists. This faith in their good sense has given many the hope and courage to act.

Joe Pearce is a person who has taken up this challenge. He has not been deterred by the fact that he is not an economist or an 'expert' in ecology, environmental science, or any other discipline that might qualify him to write this book. He has been empowered by the ideas he has found in *Small Is Beautiful* and wants others to be given the same hope that they too count and can make a difference. When *Small Is Beautiful* was first published people all over the world were inspired to change the direction of their lives in countless ways to start to build a new world. Joe's vision is that, twenty-five years later, these ideas and this inspiration should be brought to a new generation whose commitment and effort is still needed to change the world.

The world is not so different today. The problems of pollution are still with us. World poverty has not been eradicated. We have not been able to overcome our addiction to a way of life which demands high-energy consumption. Stress, drugs, crime, suicide and family breakdown have not been reduced. We need to be reminded again that we are all part of the solution, to be stirred to restore meaning to our lives and to start to live according to that meaning. I hope that all who read this book will see that small is not only still beautiful but that it is also possible. If they are then inspired to read *Small Is Beautiful* Joe will have achieved a great deal to ensure that these important ideas live on into the twenty-first century.

Barbara Wood
November 2000
Kew Gardens

1 E.F. Schumacher, *A Guide for the Perplexed,* New York: Harper and Row, 1977, p. 22.
2 E.F. Schumacher, *Small Is Beautiful: A Study of Economics As If People Mattered*, London: Blond & Briggs, 1973, p. 213.

Introduction

A STILL, SMALL VOICE

Speak through the earthquake, wind, and fire,
O still, small voice of calm!
                                    John Greenleaf Whittier (1807–82)

More than a quarter of a century ago, E.F. Schumacher rang out a timely warning to the modern world in his book *Small Is Beautiful*. Since then, millions of copies have been sold in many different languages. Few books before or since have had such a profound influence on the way the world perceives itself. Schumacher, a highly respected economist and adviser to third world governments, broke ranks with the accepted wisdom of his peers to warn of impending calamity if rampant consumerism and economic expansionism were not checked by human and environmental considerations. Like a latter-day prophet, he asserted that humanity was lurching blindly in the wrong direction, that the pursuit of wealth could not ultimately lead to happiness or fulfilment, that the pillaging of finite resources and the pollution of the planet were threatening global ecological collapse, and that a renewal of moral and spiritual perception was essential if disaster was to be avoided.

Schumacher's greatest achievement was the fusion of ancient wisdom and modern economics in a language that encapsulated contemporary doubts and fears about the industrialized world. His words resonated with echoes of Christ's Sermon on the Mount or the teachings of Buddha but always in terms that emphasized their enduring relevance. The wisdom of the ages, the perennial truth that has guided humanity throughout its history, serves as a constant reminder to each new generation of the dangers of self-gratification. The lessons of the past, if heeded, should always empower the present. But if wisdom was a warning, it was also a battle cry and a call to action. It pointed to the problem and pinpointed the solution.

As both philosopher and economist Schumacher was uniquely placed to bring the two disciplines into harmonious unity. The wide range of professional experience he had gained in the world of economics and industry was combined with his studies in philosophy so that spiritual truths and practical facts were welded into a higher realism. This led him to question many of the conventions of modern economics. For example, was big always best? Most economists, shackled to the dogmatic idolization of economies of scale, believed that the question was already answered. Even if big wasn't always best it was usually so. Mergers were considered good until or unless they led to monopoly.

Schumacher counteracted the idolatry of giantism with the beauty of smallness. People, he argued, could only feel at home in human-scale environments. If structures – economic, political or social – became too large they became impersonal and unresponsive to human needs and aspirations. Under these conditions individuals felt functionally futile, dispossessed, voiceless, powerless, excluded, alienated ... It was no coincidence that Schumacher's book was subtitled *A Study of Economics as if People Mattered.*

Real and Sub-real

Schumacher applied similar criteria with regard to technolatry, the worship of technology as intrinsically good. Modern technology, he felt, was pursuing size, speed and violence in defiance of all laws of natural harmony. The machine was becoming the master and not the servant of man, condemning humanity to an increasingly artificial existence divorced from its natural environment. Since Schumacher, the process has accelerated considerably. Reality is being replaced by virtual reality. The real is being sacrificed to the sub-real. How can humanity address the urgent problems confronting the real world when it is being simultaneously stimulated and stupefied by electronic fantasies?

One such urgent problem is technology's enormous impact on the environment. Schumacher warned that humanity could not continue to consume the planet's limited resources at the rate to which it had become accustomed, let alone increase that rate. Failure to conserve finite resources would have ultimately catastrophic effects. In this, as in so much else, Schumacher blazed a trail which others would follow. He was one of the earliest eco-warriors, and certainly one of the most influential.

In purely practical terms, Schumacher's radical ideas on the value of intermediate technology, particularly with regard to the developing countries, have also been hugely influential. As founder of the Intermediate Technology Development Group and adviser to many governments his work in this field has had continuing results. His concept of intermediate technology constituted a viable alternative to the conventional teaching of *laissez-faire* economists. The latter spoke in euphoric terms about 'stages of growth' that would lead the developing world, in the wake of western prosperity, to the same levels of high technology and high consumption. This was, in Schumacher's view, an ill-conceived and illusory vision of the future. How could countries that were desperately short of capital but endowed with an abundant and expanding labour force be expected to adopt high-cost technology, largely replacing man-power, without widespread economic and social disruption?

Instead of this inappropriate approach, Schumacher was the first western expert to argue that in areas such as India or China the prime needs, especially in rural areas where most people lived, were low-cost workplaces where capital invest-ment was kept to a minimum so that the manpower and human skills locally available could be used to the full. This intermediate, or 'appropriate', technology would conform to local requirements and facilitate socially acceptable forms of economic development.

Schumacher foresaw that the capital-intensive approach would have disastrous consequences. The investment of millions of pounds in huge high-tech plants would provide very few jobs but would leave the countries which were the recipients of such investment hugely indebted to international financial institutions. The rise of third world debt, chronic underemployment, the increasing maldistribution of income, and the flight of impoverished rural populations to lives of destitution in sprawling urban shanty-towns are all the result of inappropriate technology and investment.

Paying tribute to Schumacher shortly after his death in 1977, Barbara Ward mourned the loss of a friend 'who combined a remarkable innovating intelligence with the greatest gentleness and humour'. Significantly, she added that what the world had lost was of far greater importance. 'To very few people, it is given to begin to change, drastically and creatively, the direction of human thought. Dr Schumacher belongs to this intensely creative minority and his death is an incalculable loss to the whole international "community".'[1]

The loss, however, is not total. The remarkable innovative intelligence lingers on in his books and in the legacy of his thought. A quarter of a century after his death, Schumacher's still, small voice speaks with greater urgency than ever to a world in need of his wisdom.

The modern world enters its third millennium placing a greater burden than ever on the planet that sustains it. If it is to survive it needs the courage to look at itself in the mirror. Decisions must be made. Does humanity continue on its present path, its foot on the accelerator, in pursuit of the bigger and faster – and ultimate disaster? Or does it think again? There is a better and safer way forward. Bigger is not always best but small is still beautiful.

1 *The Times*, 10 September 1977.

PART 1

At What Price Growth?

1

Beginnings and Ends

It is hardly an exaggeration to say that, with increasing affluence, economics has moved into the very centre of public concern, and economic performance, economic growth, economic expansion, and so forth have become the abiding interest, if not the obsession, of all modern societies. In the current vocabulary of condemnation there are few words as final and conclusive as the word 'uneconomic'. If an activity has been branded as uneconomic, its right to existence is not merely questioned but energetically denied. Anything that is found to be an impediment to economic growth is a shameful thing, and if people cling to it, they are thought of as either saboteurs or fools. Call a thing immoral or ugly, soul-destroying or a degradation of man, a peril to the peace of the world or to the well-being of future generations; as long as you have not shown it to be 'uneconomic' you have not really questioned its right to exist, grow, and prosper.[1]

E.F. Schumacher

What is economics? Since that discipline was the subject of *Small Is Beautiful*, according to the book's subtitle, it is appropriate to begin by defining our terms. Yet at once we are in danger of falling into a crucial error, for economics as it is commonly defined has a different focus from that which concerns Schumacher. *Collins English Dictionary* defines the term as 'the social science concerned with the production and consumption of goods and services and the analysis of the commercial activities of a society'. According to this conventional definition, it is not people but goods and services and commercial activities that matter. But for Schumacher it is people that matter. Economics is not an end in itself but merely the means to an end determined by something other than economics. He made the revolutionary assertion that this primary truth should be the beginning and end of economics. It should have no other purpose.

People matter because they are not just matter. They are spirit; they possess a soul. This was central to Schumacher's conception of economics, as was confirmed by his choice of the following quotation from the economic historian R.H. Tawney as the epigraph at the beginning of *Small Is Beautiful*:

> *The most obvious facts are most easily forgotten. Both the existing economic order and too many of the projects advanced for reconstructing it break down through their neglect of the truism that, since even quite common men have souls, no increase in material wealth will compensate them for arrangements which insult their self-respect and impair their freedom.*

Tawney concluded with the assertion that any 'reasonable estimate of economic organization … must satisfy criteria which are not purely economic'. There was, in fact, no such thing as a purely economic problem because economics deals with human beings. Put simply, economic problems cannot be solved using purely economic methods. This conundrum was at the heart of Schumacher's book and it is the same conundrum facing any discussion of economics today.

The Death of Economics

The inability of economics to address the deepest issues of the day exposes its inadequacy and insufficiency and has caused some economists to question the very nature of their profession. Paul Ormerod studied economics at Cambridge and Oxford before becoming Head of the Economic Assessment Unit at *The Economist*. For ten years he was director of economics at the Henley Centre for Forecasting and he has been a visiting professor of economics at London and Manchester. In *The Death of Economics*[2] Ormerod exposed 'the highly tenuous nature of modern economic orthodoxy'. He argued that conventional economics offers 'a very misleading view of how the world actually operates, and that it needs to be replaced'. His fellow economists had, Ormerod wrote, 'erected around the discipline a barrier of jargon and mathematics which makes the subject difficult to penetrate for the non-initiated'. As a result, even intelligent members of the public found economics intimidating, enabling professional 'experts' to pronounce with great confidence in the media without fear of contradiction or recrimination. 'Yet orthodox economics is in many ways an empty box. Its understanding of the world is similar to that of the physical sciences in the Middle Ages. A few insights have been obtained which will stand the test of time, but they are very few indeed, and the whole basis of conventional economics is deeply flawed.'

To illustrate his point, Ormerod singles out the woeful inaccuracy of economic forecasts. In a twelve-month period in 1993–4 forecasters had failed to predict the Japanese recession, the strength of the American recovery, the depth of the collapse in the German economy and the turmoil in the European Exchange Rate Mechanism. This appalling inaccuracy on the part of economic 'experts' should have led to their forecasts becoming the subject of open derision. 'Yet to the true believers, within the profession itself, the ability of economics to understand the world has never been greater,' writes Ormerod.

There is no shortage of true believers. Economics dominates political debate to such an extent that it is almost impossible to pursue a successful political career in most western countries without being able to repeat parrot-fashion the latest fashionable economic orthodoxies. The media seek out the views of economists on Wall Street and in the City of London, anxious that the viewing public should be informed of the impact of the latest statistic on the entire economy over the coming years. With the status of economics so much in the ascendancy it is scarcely surprising that the number of career-minded students seeking to read economics grew dramatically during the 1980s and '90s.

Economics, it seems, is almost attaining pseudo-religious status, with conformity essential and heresy shunned. It has become *icon*omics, before which every knee must bend. The dissident voice of Paul Ormerod is like the lone voice in the cheering crowd who dared suggest that the emperor was wearing no clothes. Thus Ormerod exposes the naked truth: 'Good economists know, from work carried out within their discipline, that the foundations of their subject are virtually non-existent.'

Ormerod's cautionary words invite further analogies. His comparison of the position of modern economics to the

position of the physical sciences in the Middle Ages is sugges-
tive of alchemy. Both 'sciences' have, as their principal purpose,
the turning of materials, however base, into gold. Yet alchemy's
error resulted, for the most part, in a farcical waste of time and
effort, while the errors of economics could result in the waste of
the planet on which we live.

Pandora's Box

Similarly, Ormerod's suggestion that conventional economics
'is in many ways an empty box' invites comparison with the
mythical box belonging to Pandora. Indeed, such a comparison suggests that Ormerod, in this respect at least, is wrong.
Economics is not an empty box after all but, like Pandora's
box, is full of unforeseen dangers. In both cases the unwise
opening of the box has unleashed the objects of desire upon
the earth, dispersing them to play havoc among humanity
so that nothing remains except Hope. If such an analogy
appears a trifle melodramatic, a good hard look at the facts
will show that even the power of myth does not do justice to
the truth.

The unleashing of desire in the form of consumerism is
today stretching nature's tolerance to the very limits, threatening global ecological turmoil. The accelerating depletion of the
earth's finite resources to meet ever-expanding demands for
energy and consumer goods appears to be out of control.
The worship of economic growth as an end in itself is based on
the highly questionable assumption that there are no limits
to the planet's ability to sustain it. Yet none of these pressing
issues are addressed by conventional economics. It doesn't have
the answers because it doesn't even ask the questions. It is an
apt and amusing irony that the phrase 'to be economical with

the truth' has become associated with distorting reality or telling lies. To amend a well-worn cliché, there are lies, damned lies and conventional economics.

1 E.F. Schumacher, *Small Is Beautiful*, London: Abacus, 1973, p. 34.
2 Paul Ormerod, *The Death of Economics*, London: Faber and Faber, 1994.

2

Malignant Growth

The real issue – or, to be more precise, the issue that I regard as dominant today – is whether we are ready seriously to recognize that the collective pursuit of economic growth, which depends, in the main, on scientific advance and technological progress, has begun to have complex and far-reaching consequences both on the biosphere and on the 'sociosphere', consequences that are by no means entirely benign. They demand the most searching study and surmise. For it is now reasonable to believe that, despite the abundance of man-made goods produced by continued economic growth, its net effect on human health and happiness could be adverse and possibly disastrous.[1]

E.J. Mishan

In his book *Phases of Capitalist Development*,[2] Angus Maddison charts the growth of what are now the western economies over the past fifteen hundred years. He estimates that during the thousand years between AD 500 and 1500, gross domestic product (GDP)[3] grew on average by only 0.1 per cent a year. As such, the volume of economic activity in 1500 was between 2.5 and 3 times as great as it had been a thousand years earlier.

To put this in perspective, the western economies grew as much in percentage terms in the twenty years between 1950 and 1970 as they had done in the thousand years between 500 and 1500. And, of course, the much higher base at the start of the 1950s means that the absolute increase in goods and services was enormously greater. Today the growth of world GDP regularly exceeds 3 per cent per annum.[4]

Growth began to accelerate around 1500, and between then and 1700 Maddison estimates that total economic output almost doubled. The acceleration continued and throughout the eighteenth century annual growth was over 0.5 per cent a year, with the more active economies, such as Britain, experiencing growth of the order of a full 1 per cent a year. Such growth was dramatic. Major changes were experienced in a single lifetime, placing enormous pressure on cultural tradition and giving added impetus to the notion of 'progress'. Economic growth both caused and exceeded the surge in population, ensuring that relative material prosperity for some was accompanied by major social upheaval for others. The sheer magnitude of the growth was without precedent in human history, and it was only just getting started.

By the end of the eighteenth century, the industrial revolution had hardly begun. Its impact throughout the nineteenth century not only ensured that the pace of growth accelerated as never before, but facilitated, through the expansion of the British Empire, a huge increase in the flow of trade around the world. The process of globalization had commenced on a scale that would have been inconceivable to previous generations. This process gained momentum at the end of the nineteenth century with the emergence of the United States as a major economic force.

In 1870 the population of America was thirty-nine million, eight million more than the population of Britain at the time.

Income per head in America was about eighty per cent of that in Britain. The combination of a higher population and a lower income per head meant that the size of the American domestic market was very similar to that of the British. Yet by the beginning of the First World War, less than half a century later, the United States had overtaken its main competitor. Instead of its average income being twenty per cent lower than that in Britain it was now twenty per cent higher. Instead of their domestic markets being in virtual equity the American market had become two and a half times larger than the British.

Why did the United States rise to a position of global economic dominance? There is no doubt that technological advances, such as the expansion of the railways and the invention of the telegraph, played an important part in continuing and accelerating economic growth but these advances were applicable to the economies of both the United States and Europe. In large part America's new position was due to the rapid rise in the US population, and therefore the rapid growth of its domestic market, but it was helped considerably by a particular piece of legislation that would determine the shape and size of American industry – the Sherman Antitrust Act.

During the 1870s and 1880s many manufacturers in both Europe and America formed trade associations, the purpose of which was to allow companies to control markets and fix prices so that profits could be maximized. In America the US Congress responded by passing the 1890 Sherman Antitrust Act, which declared such associations to be illegal. The passing of this act in America, and the absence of anything similar in Europe, was to tip the scales of advantage firmly in America's favour: not, however, because the act succeeded but because it failed. Large companies simply outmanoeuvred the legislation by formalizing the illegal associations through legal mergers and acquisitions. The results were revolutionary. Before the act a large number of small and medium-size companies had worked together to control the market; after the act a small number of large companies simply swallowed up their smaller rivals, destroying the competition and gaining an even tighter control of the market than before.

Birth of the Big

The Antitrust Act was hugely influential to the future development of the world economy. It gave birth to the Big as a major economic power, and smothered the Small. Like a Sherman tank it rolled relentlessly across the economic landscape. By the turn of the century the merger and acquisition movement was unstoppable, laying the foundation for America's economic supremacy. Companies of enormous size dominated and outgrew the domestic economy, seeking opportunities to make inroads into foreign markets. The age of the multinational had arrived.

This potted history of economic development over the past fifteen hundred years raises an obvious question. Is the process of unprecedented and accelerating economic growth benign or malignant? Almost without exception, the world's economists, lining up rank upon rank, will sing in chorus that economic growth is overwhelmingly beneficial. Any problems caused by such growth are outweighed by the enormous benefits accrued to mankind by the added wealth it produces.

Superficially at least, this appears to be a persuasive argument. Few would dispute that most people in the 'developed' world are better off in monetary terms or in terms of the number of things they possess. The problem arises once one goes deeper than the monetary or the material. Other questions must be asked before a judgement can be reached on the benefits or otherwise of economic growth, for example:

- What is wealth?
- Is it quantitative or qualitative?
- If it is qualitative, can it be measured economically?
- If it is quantitative, what does wealth cost? Does it cost more than it is worth?
- Does money buy happiness?
- Can material possessions prevent personal sorrow or suffering?
- Does everything have its price, or are some things priceless?
- Is there a difference between price and value? If there is, does price distort value?

At root the problem lies with the mechanistic materialism of most economists. Implicitly at least, they work on the assumption that, as a general rule, if someone is ten per cent richer in monetary terms, they will be approximately ten per cent happier. Therefore, by implication, if economic growth brings extra material wealth it will bring extra happiness. Is this so?

The Paradox of Prosperity

In the early seventies Professor Richard Easterlin compared the results of public opinion surveys in the United States.[5] He concluded that there was no clear relationship between average per capita income and the degree of happiness. On the contrary, most Americans, on balance, believed themselves to be less happy in 1970 than they were in 1957. In the years since Easterlin's work many other studies have reached similar conclusions. In late 1999 a report from the Henley Centre, entitled *The Paradox of Prosperity*, concluded that rising prosperity in the new millennium would be accompanied by worsening social upheaval. There would be more broken marriages, worsening drug dependency, higher levels of workplace stress and increased loneliness. In short, the paradox of prosperity was that more money meant more misery. Such evidence is, of course, open to misinterpretation and abuse. As with most statistics, its use is limited and should not be overstated. Yet similar studies, before and since, continue to question seriously whether there can be any reliable correlation between happiness and material wealth. At the very least, the whole concept is open to debate.

The question of economic growth is thrown into further confusion by the methods used to measure it. Fundamentally, economics is myopic. It measures reality by its current market price. The intrinsic value of real things, their essential character which remains unchanged even when their price on the market fluctuates, is not an issue to the economist. He is, like Oscar Wilde's cynic, someone who knows the price of everything and the value of nothing. Forced by his own preconceptions to keep a watchful eye on current market forces, he is consigned permanently to the present, spurning both the past and the future. Henry Ford, that great champion of industrialism, expressed his contempt for the past by dismissing all history as 'bunk'. Meanwhile, the celebrated economist John Maynard Keynes exemplified the emphasis on the short as opposed to the long term in economic judgements with the cheerfully brutal reminder that in the long term we are all dead. The conservation of our natural and cultural heritage, and the future destiny of unborn generations, are scarcely in safe hands where such short-sightedness holds sway.

The myopic nature of modern economics was stressed by Schumacher when he insisted that there can be 'no doubt whatever' about the fragmentary nature of economic judgements. Apart from the perennial preoccupation with short-term considerations, he pointed out that the judgements of economics were based on a definition of cost which excluded all 'free goods', i.e., to use Schumacher's own definition, 'the entire God-given environment, except for those parts of it that have been privately appropriated'. In other words, any activity can be deemed 'economic', even if it seriously pollutes the environment, as long as it shows a profit, whereas a competing activity which, at some cost, protects and conserves the environment, will be 'uneconomic' if its profits are lower. The profit motive, enshrined as the profit imperative, leads to an inherent flaw in the methodology of economics that results in the failure to recognize humanity's ultimate dependence on the natural world. This aspect of economic short-sightedness is discussed at greater length in the next chapter.

True Value

Price-worship has also blinded economists to the true value of the goods being priced. In modern economics any distinction between categories of goods refers only to their place in the market. Thus modern economics only makes a distinction from the point of view of the purchaser, such as the distinction between consumers' goods and producers' goods. Economists consider that goods are only there for the buying; no account is taken of their being – what they actually are. This is not purely a question of semantics. Major problems arise if no account is taken of whether goods are man-made or God-given, whether they are renewable or otherwise.

Schumacher distinguishes between primary, or God-given, goods and secondary, or man-made, goods. He then distinguishes between renewable and non-renewable primary goods and between the two distinct categories of secondary goods, i.e. manufactures and services. This, he says, is a minimum scheme of categorization of goods. The categories are numbered as follows: (1) non-renewable primary goods, (2) renewable primary goods, (3) manufactured secondary goods, and (4) services. These differences between the various categories of goods cannot be disregarded without losing touch with reality. Since man is not a producer but only a converter, or, as others have preferred to say, because he is not a creator but only a sub-creator, he cannot make something out of nothing. Consequently, secondary goods are utterly dependent on primary goods. Man's ability to bring forth secondary goods – manufactures and services – depends on his ability to obtain primary goods from the earth. These primary goods, the raw materials for secondary production, can be either renewable or non-renewable.

This may all sound pretty obvious, yet the market is blind to such distinctions. It puts a price tag on all goods, indiscriminately eliminating value. Fifty pounds' worth of oil (category 1) equals fifty pounds' worth of cotton (category 2) equals fifty pounds' worth of clothes (category 3) equals fifty pounds' worth of hotel accommodation (category 4). There is no difference between any of these goods, as far as the market is concerned, except in the profit margins that can be obtained by providing them. If a greater profit can be made from categories 3 and 4 than from categories 1 and 2 it will be 'economic' to switch resources from the latter to the former.

The most fundamental flaw in the way that economic growth is measured is linked inextricably to the worship of the price mechanism. The slavery of economists to the omnipotent Market has resulted in their linking the rate of growth to 'gross national product' (GNP). If gross national product increases there is growth in the economy. And, since growth is always considered good, the more that GNP increases the more economists will speak of a 'healthy economy' and the more politicians will preen themselves on their success in bringing it about. Yet measuring the rate of growth in terms of GNP is very misleading, as Richard Douthwaite illustrated with great clarity in *The Growth Illusion*.[6]

GNP is the total price (not value, since value is qualitative not quantitative) of all the traded goods and services produced in a country during a year. Any economic activity that does not involve a monetary transaction is not included. On the other hand, any activity that involves the spending of money is included even if it has a detrimental effect in socio-economic terms. This produces a peculiar view of what is deemed 'economic'.

'Uneconomic' Economies

Preparing meals at home is less 'economic' than eating at a restaurant because the latter activity contributes more to GNP. Similarly, all do-it-yourself economies around the home or on the car are in fact 'uneconomic' because more economic growth would be recorded if everyone employed builders or garages to do the work. Caring for elderly or disabled people at home within a loving family environment, where they are largely invisible economically, is less 'economic' than having their 'price' measured in a nursing home.

In short, the more people are self-sufficient and not reliant on others, the less they are considered 'economic'. The more they are dependent on others the higher will be their contribution to

GNP. The absurdity of this state of affairs was illustrated by Alvin Toffler in *The Third Wave*:

> With respect to the pursuit of GNP, an amusing fantasy suggests that women undertake to do each other's housework and pay each other for it. If every Susie Smith paid every Barbara Brown one hundred dollars a week for caring for her home and children, while receiving an equivalent amount for providing the same services in return, the impact on the Gross National Product would be astounding. If fifty million American housewives engaged in this nonsense transaction it would add about ten per cent to the US GNP overnight.[7]

Since GNP is purely quantitative it makes no allowance for the quality of life. Clean air, silence, natural beauty, self-respect, simplicity, the love within families, and the value of relationships between people are of no relevance to the concept of economic growth. In fact, since growth in GNP demands as much economic activity as possible it puts a strain on each of these causes of happiness. A family which is self-sufficient in many of its domestic activities, whose members enjoy the simple pleasures in life without recourse to expensive and artificial technological stimulants, may be happy people but they are bad consumers. They are not contributing 'healthily' to the growth of GNP.

The ramifications are obvious. Since economic growth needs good consumers it will court those in the population who are restless, dissatisfied, and who are in need of artificial stimulants to cheer up their lives. Someone who is contented will not want more, or not enough more. Someone who is discontented will always want more, or can always be persuaded that they want more, and they will never have enough. The next purchase only brings instant gratification, not long-term satisfaction, so that they are soon looking for the next purchase, the next instant gratification. James D. Schwartz, an American planning consultant, referred to consumers with this 'more and onwards' mentality as 'more-ons'.[8]

'More-onic'

The logical absurdity of the 'more-onic' approach is that, according to GNP-linked measurements of growth, a person who economizes behaves uneconomically. He is bad for business. One could be forgiven for believing that the real had become surreal or that sense had become nonsense. The world of economics resembles a Mad Hatter's tea-party where all the crockery is smashed at the end of festivities so that the economy can be boosted by the necessity of buying a whole new tea-set. In fact conventional economics already has a name for such a necessity. It is called built-in obsolescence.

The problem is that economic growth, as measured by the increase in the gross national product, has precious little to do with people's wealth or well-being. It merely records activity. If a major calamity occurs, such as a hurricane or an earthquake, there might be a growth in GNP because activity is increased to repair the damage. If there is a major ecological disaster, such as the Exxon Valdez oil spill, it will appear in the national income statistics as an increase in GNP because of the enormous spending necessary in the clean-up operation. If the crime rate increases, GNP records economic growth because more people are employed in the police force, more prisons are built, and more is spent on insurance and personal security. Of course, this kind of spending, even if good for GNP statistics, will eventually lead a country to bankruptcy.

Perhaps the most striking example is that of the tobacco industry. First, there is the huge profit made by the tobacco companies. Second, there are the billions made by governments in the levying of taxes on cigarettes. Both contribute enormously to growth in GNP and, therefore, according to economists, to the economic welfare of the community. So far, so questionable. But this is only half the story. In the early 1990s the cost of cancer in the United States alone was estimated at $110 billion per annum.[9] Common sense would suggest that this cost should be set against the profits of the tobacco companies and the increased revenue of governments who raise taxes through the sale of cigarettes. Not in the least. The construction of new hospitals and the employment of public health workers all add to GNP, making us 'wealthier'. The $110 billion per annum attributed to cancer in the US was equal to 1.7 per cent of GNP. Do cigarettes make people 1.7 per cent happier? Does cancer?

Similar examples could be given. Drug abuse, for instance, has extra economic benefits. Not only is there the 'wealth' created by the medical care needed for drug abusers, there is also the economic growth caused by the social care needed for their rehabilitation, and the 'prosperity' caused by the thousands of police employed in tackling the supply of drugs. Unfortunately, the drug dealers themselves are part of the black economy and so their profits are not recorded in the GNP. Fortunately, however, the money they spend as good consumers on expensive products helps to bolster economic growth. And, of course, by legalizing drugs the government could bolster GNP by ensuring that the dealers were shown statistically to be benefiting the economy. The government would be enabled to tax drug use, boosting economic growth still further. Finally, if legalization led to a dramatic increase in the use of drugs the added health and social care required would be an added bonus to the nation's economic 'well-being', while eventually bankrupting the public purse.

The cost of drug abuse in the US in the early 1990s was $200 billion, or 3.1 per cent of GNP;[10] the cost of crime was $163 billion, or 2.6 per cent of GNP.[11] In other words, cancer, drug abuse and crime contributed $473 billion, 7.4 per cent, towards the GNP of the United States. And all three areas are not only growing, but are boom industries.

Admittedly these are extreme examples but they serve to illustrate the degree to which GNP confounds any true estimate of wealth or well-being in society. They show that gross national product represents a gross, irrational distortion. The growth it measures is often malignant and it is worshipped by those who know how to count but have forgotten how to see. They have forgotten that it is not the quantity of things possessed but the quality of life lived that matters.

1 E.J. Mishan, *The Economic Growth Debate*, London: George Allen & Unwin, 1977.
2 Angus Maddison, *Phases of Capitalist Development*, Oxford University Press, 1982.
3 The total value of all goods and services produced by a nation during a year, equivalent to gross national product (GNP) minus net investment incomes from foreign nations.
4 International Monetary Fund, *World Economic Outlook*, 1996.
5 Cited in Mishan, *The Economic Growth Debate*, p. 25.
6 Richard Douthwaite, *The Growth Illusion*, Bideford, Devon: Green Books, 1992.
7 Alvin Toffler, *The Third Wave*, New York: Bantam Press edn., 1981, pp. 450–1.
8 James D. Schwartz, 'More versus Enough: Aligning Life Goals with Personal Financial Resources', 1986, unpublished manuscript.
9 *Los Angeles Times*, 8 September 1993.

10 R. Godson and W. Olson, *International Organized Crime: Emerging Threat to US Security*, Washington: National Strategy Information Center, August 1993.
11 *Washington Post*, 6 July 1994.

3

Expand and Die

Looking outward to the blackness of space I can see majesty but no welcome ... but below me is a welcoming planet. There, contained in the thin, moving, incredibly fragile shell of the biosphere is everything that is dear to me, all the human drama and comedy. That's where life is; that's where all the good stuff is.

Loren Acton (astronaut)

Loren Acton's words from the Challenger space shuttle to NASA's mission control in July 1985 are a poignant reminder of the 'incredibly fragile shell' that protects all life on earth. Similar sentiments have been expressed by other astronauts. Ulf Merbold spoke of seeing the horizon for the first time as a curved line: 'It was accentuated by a thin seam of dark blue light – our atmosphere. Obviously this was not the ocean of air I had been told it was so many times in my life. I was terrified by its fragile appearance.'

Aleksandr Aleksandrov, a cosmonaut on the Soviet Soyuz T-9 in June 1983, described the warmth he felt towards mother earth when looking upon her from space. His words accentuated the ethical bankruptcy of the Cold War and the folly of the nuclear catastrophe it threatened to unleash upon the planet. 'It struck me that we are all children of our Earth. It does not matter what country you look at. We are all Earth's children and should treat her as our mother.' Perhaps, however, the most romantically allusive description was given by the American astronaut James Irwin:

> The Earth reminded us of a Christmas tree ornament hanging in the blackness of space. As we got farther and farther away it diminished in size. Finally it shrank to the size of a marble, the most beautiful marble you can imagine. That beautiful, warm, living object looked so fragile, so delicate, that if you touched it with a finger it would crumble and fall apart. Seeing this has to change a man…

If the view from the perspective of space presents a picture of a frighteningly fragile planet, the view from the perspective of time is even more alarming. The earth is approximately 4,600 million years old. Since it is hard to imagine such an age, it is helpful to use a well-known analogy. If we compare the life of the earth with the life of a man, and make one hundred thousand million earth-years equivalent to one man-year, a shocking reality emerges. Today, the man would be forty-six years old. For the first forty or so years of his life there was no life on earth. The earth began to flower only four years ago when the man was forty-two. For the last four years the earth has blossomed into an Eden-like garden of multifarious flora and fauna. Dinosaurs first appeared a year ago. Modern man was born only four hours ago. In the last hour he discovered agriculture. It is only in the last minute that humanity has left its mark on the world. Since then, whole civilizations have risen and fallen in a few seconds.

Techno-man

Civilized man has now been replaced by techno-man, who is bringing the planet to the edge of the abyss. In the last second or so of earth time we have ripped a hole in the delicate fabric that wraps the earth. The hole in the ozone layer, visible from space, is the result of the pollution caused by humanity in the blink of an eye. The paradise presented to humankind is being destroyed at an alarming speed. Our lifestyle and high consumption rate have all but drained the world's resources. The results include water shortages, land degradation, tropical forest destruction, species extinction, overfishing, and urban air pollution in many of the world's mega-cities. Since 1970 we have destroyed nearly half the natural world. Under such pressure, the delicate planet on which we live has reached crisis point. The earth's ecosystem is in danger of collapse.

Ultimately small is beautiful because the earth itself is not only beautiful but small. Technology has made it possible for humanity to exploit the earth's limited resources to such an extent that humanity's appetite for growth has outstripped the planet's ability to satisfy it. Human beings cannot take more from the earth than the earth is capable of giving. Techno-man is in danger of exploiting himself to extinction.

There is, of course, a link between the bigger picture presented here and the smaller picture exhibited at the beginning of the previous chapter. This potted history of the planet is akin to observing the problem through a telescope, whereas the potted history of the economy given in chapter 2 is akin to examining the same problem under a microscope. It is only through examining the picture under a microscope that the germ of the problem can be discovered.

Growth Imperative

The man-made bacterium that threatens the life of the planet is the growth imperative at the heart of modern economics. This owes its existence in large part to the debt to which economic activity is subject. When a company or a government borrows money the debt can be paid only in one of two ways: either by taking the money from salaries or savings, i.e. by self-sacrifice, or by ensuring sufficient growth to cover the cost of repayment. Naturally, the latter option is considered preferable. Thus the burden of debt carried by the economy necessitates economic growth at all costs. It is for this reason that economists and politicians consider growth in GNP so important. Increasing economic activity means that the economy can continue to chase its debt.

Yet such is the nature of the system that the debt is not reduced. Growth requires further investment which necessitates further borrowing, and borrowing in turn requires further growth. It is a vicious circle. 'In our present economic system,' the economist and writer Richard Douthwaite observed, 'the choice is between growth and collapse, not growth and stability.'[1] It was for this reason that Edward Heath, former British Prime Minister, once remarked that 'the alternative to expansion is not an England of quiet market towns linked only by trains puffing slowly and peacefully through green meadows. The alternative is slums, dangerous roads, old factories, cramped schools, and stunted lives.'[2]

The 'expand or die' mentality of modern economists and politicians was exemplified in September 1999 by Britain's Chancellor of the Exchequer, Gordon Brown. In an upbeat and triumphalist assessment of the economy, Brown announced that Britain was on the verge of an era of high economic growth similar to that experienced by the United States in the 1990s. He told an audience in New York that 'the opportunity now exists in Britain for a new virtuous cycle of low inflation, high investment and high and stable levels of growth'.[3] The response to the Chancellor's triumphalism varied. His colleagues in the Labour government claimed that high economic growth was the result of government policy. Meanwhile, his opponents in the Conservative party claimed that high levels of growth were only possible because of the deregulation and privatization introduced by the previous Tory government. Many economists believed that increased growth had very little to do with the policies of either party but was the result of the so-called New Paradigm, the theory that constant economic growth was due to technological advances such as the Internet. Whatever their differences, all agreed that economic growth was desirable. Indeed, the Chancellor went even further, declaring that growth was not merely desirable but 'virtuous', bestowing it with a moral rectitude and purity.

On the very day that Gordon Brown was basking in the glories of growth, a United Nations report exposed the horrifying costs of his 'virtuous' system. *GEO-2000*, the Global Environment Outlook report published by the UN Environment Programme,[4] warned that it was too late to stop the first stages of global warming, the destruction of thousands of the world's species, or prevent shortages of water across swathes of Africa and Asia that could provoke wars in the first quarter-century of the new millennium. The wasteful consumer society in rich countries had combined with rapid population growth in the third world to attack the earth's finite resources in a deadly pincer movement. According to the United Nations, the combined effect of this attack on Mother Earth had suicidal consequences for humanity. It was threatening to destroy the natural resources on which human life depended.

'Full-scale Emergencies'

GEO-2000 pinpointed 'full-scale emergencies' in several areas devastated by the adverse effects of growth. Specifically, many areas of the world would begin to run out of fresh water over the next twenty-five years, raising the prospect of 'water wars' fought for the remaining scarce resources in areas as diverse as North Africa, the Middle East and Asia. Commenting on deforestation, the report disclosed that 80 per cent of the world's original forest cover had been cleared, fragmented or degraded. Seventy per cent of the forest had gone in Asia and the earth was losing an area of forest the size of England and Wales every year. It would take generations to repair the damage done to the forests, assuming that present destructive trends could be reversed. The cultures that had lived in them for thousands of years, however, were now lost forever.

There was a global nitrogen pollution problem caused by fertilizers and by the burning of fossil fuels. Some areas were now contaminated by nitrogen compounds to such a level that water supplies could become unfit for human consumption. Nitrogen contamination in these areas could also cause excessive algal growth which would destroy wildlife.

Many of the planet's species had been lost or were now condemned to extinction because of the slow response of politicians in tackling environmental degradation. One quarter of the world's mammal species were now at significant risk of extinction. It was now too late to preserve all the biodiversity that enriched the planet. Land degradation had reduced the fertility of the soil and marine fisheries were being 'grossly over-exploited'. Levels of fishing had almost doubled and the United Nations estimated that 60 per cent of the world's fisheries were either fully exploited or in decline.

The UNEP's director, Klaus Topfer, emphasized that time was running out if the major ecological problems facing the world were to be tackled. Dr Topfer said that many countries would fail to meet the targets for preventing man-made climate change set at Kyoto in 1997, dooming the world to an average temperature rise of up to 3 degrees Celsius during the next century. 'I am not being pessimistic,' he added, 'just realistic.'

Dr Topfer's scepticism that industrialized countries would meet the target of an overall 5 per cent reduction on 1990 emissions set at Kyoto was due in large part to the inaction of the United States. America was the world's largest emitter of carbon dioxide yet the US Senate had refused to ratify the treaty. Furthermore, in March 2001, President George W. Bush resolutely rejected the Kyoto agreement, prompting environmentalists to dub him the 'Toxic Texan'. Bush's stance on global warming, due no doubt to his background as an oil prospector in West Texas, had sounded the death knell for Kyoto. 'The Kyoto treaty's immediate impact on climate change may be slight,' conceded Roger Higman of Friends of the Earth, 'but it has always been seen as the first of a series of climate deals. The disaster of Mr Bush's announcement is that, without the first deal, further deals cannot even be debated.'[5] A similarly pessimistic assessment was offered by Dr Tim Green of the School of Environment Science at the University of East Anglia: 'Allowing economic growth to take precedence over environmental issues is a high-risk strategy in the long term, so it is hardly surprising that short-term politicians use this to their advantage.'[6]

'It is absolutely crucial to give more thought to the future,' Dr Topfer urged. 'Human activities have grown to the point where they affect the large-scale physical systems of the planet and present-day actions will have consequences that reach far into the future. We can no longer be complacent and assume that the environment can look after itself."[7]

A New Kind of Growth

Clearly the *GEO-2000* report throws into question the whole concept of economic growth and development. It is for this reason that the worship of continuous growth has been called the ideology of the cancer cell. Paradoxically, however, even Schumacher believed that there must be growth. Without growth there is stagnation. The key question is what kind of growth? Schumacher employed an analogy. Whereas physical growth is good in the case of a child, further physical growth is undesirable once the child has developed to its adult size. An adult, who cannot grow taller, can only get fatter. Consequently a new kind of growth needs to take place if healthy development is to continue. Healthy growth cannot be external or physical so it must be an inner metaphysical growth. Unfortunately, the materialist ethos of the modern world prevents the inner growth that would enable it to develop culturally or spiritually. It merely becomes physically obese, burgeoning outwards. Unwilling to become fitter, it simply becomes fatter. Economically speaking, though hardly in terms of faith or culture, the developed world should be called the over-developed world.

The pressures being put on the planet by the greed of the over-developed world are being exacerbated by the needs of the developing countries. The world's population has now topped six billion and most of the dramatic population growth is in the poorest parts of the world. In the 1950s the population of Africa was a third that of Europe. Now it is about the same. Africa's population now grows by nearly two million every month. By 2050, if present trends continue, it is predicted that the population of Europe will be only a third the size of Africa's. And what is true of Africa is true of other parts of the developing world. The population of Vietnam is increasing by more than a million every eight months, that of the Philippines increases by a million every seven and a half months, and Indonesia's population grows by a million every four months.

Over a third of the world's population lives in just two countries – China and India. A look at the burgeoning population growth in each of these will illustrate graphically the scale of the problem confronting humanity. In 1901 the population of present-day India was 238 million with an annual growth rate of 0.3 per cent; by 1931 it had reached 279 million with an annual growth rate of 1 per cent. In the past fifty years the rate of growth has accelerated and since 1961 it has consistently topped 2 per cent per annum. By 1991 the population had reached 844 million, growing to beyond a billion at the turn of the millennium.[8]

Contrary to ill-informed prejudice in over-developed countries, this population growth is not due to excessive birth rates – which are falling consistently – but to dramatic drops in the death rate. In 1901 the crude birth rate in India was 45.8 per thousand, compared with a crude death rate of 44.4 per thousand. Thus the annual growth rate was only 0.3 per cent. By 1991 the crude birth rate had dropped to 34.2 per thousand whereas the death rate had reduced to only 11.5 per thousand, increasing the annual growth rate to 2.3 per cent.[9]

The demographic history of China parallels the accelerated growth experienced in India. It is thought that China's population was about seventy million at the time of Christ. From then until the seventeenth century it remained fairly stable, fluctuating between around fifty and a hundred million. In the mid-1770s, with the establishment of the Ching dynasty, China's population began to increase dramatically. From around 100 million in 1770 it had reached 400 million by 1840. Population growth then slowed down. By the birth of the People's Republic of China in 1949 the population exceeded 500 million. After this date the population rocketed. Between 1949 and 1984 it doubled to more than a billion. The results of China's fourth national population census, conducted in 1990, shows a population of 1.13 billion.[10]

The population explosion in India, China and other parts of the developing world is reflected in world population figures. In the first century AD it is estimated that the world's population was around 170 million. By the end of the first millennium it had risen to around 265 million. Five hundred years later it had reached 425 million. It was from around this time that levels of growth began to accelerate at an increasingly dramatic pace. Within three hundred years the global population had doubled. In 1800 it is estimated to have been around 900 million. In a little over a century it had doubled again, reaching two billion by 1930. In forty years it had once again doubled, topping four billion by 1970. Thirty years later and the figure has increased to six billion.

Taking the overall picture of the growth in the world's population, it is intriguing to note the extent to which its acceleration mirrors the accelerated growth of the over-developed economies (see chapter 2). This is no coincidence. International financial institutions, multinational corporations and national governments have all contrived to incorporate the third world into the expanding world economy. So far, their efforts have not benefited the bulk of the population in the poorest countries. In many cases, such attempts have served only to impoverish them still further. The introduction of inappropriate technology in third world countries has forced many millions to uproot themselves from villages and migrate to the cities, where they are doomed to lives of urban squalor and deprivation. This, however, is only half the story. Once they arrive in the expanding third world mega-cities, these displaced millions are contributing significantly to the global ecological crisis. The *GEO-2000* report singles out the mega-cities of the developing world as major pollutants of the earth's atmosphere. Urban air pollution in these cities has been reaching 'crisis proportions', contributing to global warming and causing major health problems to many millions in the cities themselves.

Those who subscribe to the expand-or-die policies of modern economics prefer to ignore such problems. Such 'temporary difficulties', though regrettable, are dismissed as the painful but necessary labour pains that precede the birth of a brave new world of prosperity which will enrich the whole of the world's population. Apologists for global consumerism paint rosy pictures of the world as a global village united in its love for consumer goods. We are all one because we all buy the same trademarked products. The future is bright, the future is … (insert the name of your favourite brand). This is the happy ending which awaits the world if market forces are allowed to prevail. Those who disagree are dismissed as prophets of doom.

Success Guarantees Failure

Unfortunately, this wishful example of 'positive thinking' contains a fatal flaw, namely that its success guarantees its failure. As Schumacher observed: 'Modern man does not experience himself as a part of nature but as an outside force destined to dominate and conquer it. He even talks of a battle with nature, forgetting that, if he won the battle, he would find himself on the losing side.'[11]

If the globalist dream is fulfilled, it must surely mean that the whole of the world's population will enjoy the fruits of the consumer system. Imagine everyone in China owning two cars. Imagine everyone in India demanding the same number of consumer goods as the average American. Several billion extra cars polluting the atmosphere, hundreds of thousands of new factories producing hundreds of billions of disposable goods for the billions of new consumers in the developing world. The economist's dream is the ecologist's nightmare.

There is a mathematical proverb about a frog which is placed in the middle of a table. Each time the frog leaps towards the edge of the table it jumps half as far as it did the time before. If its first leap takes it half way to the table's edge, how long will it take the frog to jump off the table? The answer, of course, is that the frog will never reach the edge. But what if the frog jumps not half as far each time but twice as far? How long will it take the frog to jump off the table's edge? Regardless of how small is its first leap or how large is the table, it will take the proverbial frog no time at all to leap over the edge.

Moving from proverbial truth to anecdotal fact, Schumacher told an amusing story of an encounter with an economist from an Iron Curtain country during the Cold War period. This economist said to Schumacher that 'the west is like an express train hurtling ever faster towards an abyss … But we shall overtake them!'

Conventional economics is powerless to address the urgency of the issues facing humanity. Economic 'realism' dictates that the world economy must expand or die. Yet economic 'realism' is on a collision course with ecological reality. In the real world, as opposed to the utopian dreams of consumerism, expand *or* die translates simply as expand *and* die.

1 Douthwaite, *The Growth Illusion*, p. 20.
2 Quoted in Douthwaite, *The Growth Illusion*, p. 20.
3 *Daily Telegraph*, 16 September 1999.
4 See the *GEO-2000* report published by the UN Environment Programme, September 1999.
5 *Daily Telegraph*, 31 March 2001.
6 Ibid.
7 Ibid.
8 G. Narayana and John F. Kantner, *Doing the Needful: The Dilemma of India's Population Policy*, Oxford: Westview Press, 1992, pp. 20–1; Roger Jeffery and Patricia Jeffery, *Population, Gender and Politics: Demographic Change in Rural North India*, Cambridge University Press, 1997, p. 48.
9 Ibid.
10 Dudley L. Poston, Jr. and David Yankey (eds.), *The Population of Modern China*, New York: Plenum Press, 1992, pp. 1–2.
11 Schumacher, *Small Is Beautiful*, pp. 10–11.

PART 2

Economics and the Soul

4

The Cost of Free Trade

It is not the fundamental reason in things that is at fault; it is a particular hitch or falsification, arising from a very recent trick of regarding everything only in relation to trade. Trade is all very well in its way, but Trade has been put in the place of Truth. Trade, which is in its nature a secondary or dependent thing, has been treated as a primary and independent thing; as an absolute. The moderns, mad upon mere multiplication, have even made a plural out of what is essentially singular, in the sense of single. They have taken what all ancient philosophers called the Good, and translated it as the Goods.

G.K. Chesterton

The refusal of the US Senate to ratify the treaty signed at Kyoto was only the latest in a string of obstructive measures on the part of the American government to hamper efforts to reduce world pollution levels. As the United States is the world's largest emitter of carbon dioxide, the US government's intransigence has jeopardized efforts to achieve a 5 per cent reduction in greenhouse gas emissions. This is ecologically irresponsible considering America's major role in creating the very problem that its politicians continually choose to ignore.

In 1973 Schumacher highlighted the cost to the rest of the world of carrying the burden of the American dream. The 5.6 per cent of the world's population that lived in the United States required something of the order of 40 per cent of the world's primary resources to keep going. Schumacher then quoted Professor Walter Heller, a former adviser to the US President, who stated that America needed continued economic growth: 'We need expansion to fulfil our nation's aspirations ... I cannot conceive a successful economy without growth.' 'But,' Schumacher replied, 'if the United States' economy cannot conceivably be successful without further rapid growth, and if that growth depends on being able to draw ever-increasing resources from the rest of the world, what about the other 94.4 per cent of mankind which are so far "behind" America?' Almost thirty years on, Schumacher's question remains unanswered.

At around the same time that Schumacher's *Small Is Beautiful* was being written, a study group at the Massachusetts Institute of Technology produced a groundbreaking report entitled *The Limits to Growth*. Among its many findings, the extent to which the US economy was pillaging the planet's primary resources was of particular interest. It emerged that the US was by far the greatest consumer of the nineteen non-renewable natural materials of vital importance to industrial societies. US consumption as a percentage of the world total was as follows: aluminium, 42 per cent; chromium, 19 per cent; coal, 44 per cent; cobalt, 32 per cent; copper, 33 per cent; gold, 26 per cent; iron, 28 per cent; lead, 25 per cent; manganese, 14 per cent; mercury, 24 per cent; molybdenum, 40 per cent; natural gas, 63 per cent; nickel, 38 per cent; petroleum, 33 per cent; platinum group, 31 per cent; silver, 26 per cent; tin, 24 per cent; tungsten, 22 per cent; zinc, 26 per cent.

These figures are now out of date, but they illustrate a timely truth. The United States is still the greatest consumer of the earth's primary resources. More recent figures[1] show that the per capita consumption of energy in the US was 10,127 kilograms of coal equivalent, more than double that of other industrial countries such as Japan (4,032) and dozens of times greater than poor countries like India (307) and Bangladesh (69). The stark reality is that the average American uses thirty-three times as much energy as the average Indian and almost 150 times as much as the average person in Bangladesh. The richest 10 per cent of Americans pump eleven tons of carbon dioxide per individual into the atmosphere annually, more than a hundred times more than the poor in the developing countries. In the future, if US consumption in relation to the rest of the world drops, it will not be due to America using less but to other parts of the world using more. In the past thirty years, as other economies have joined the scramble for fast-track economic growth, more countries have begun demanding their own share of the earth's disappearing resources.

The Micawber Factor

The response to figures such as these by conventional economists is interesting. The optimistic school insist that there is no need for alarm. They are sure that the earth's crust must contain much more than has thus far been discovered. Science will always find ways of discovering and extracting further supplies of key resources before any serious shortage occurs. New technology will ensure that demand will always be met by an adequate supply, or, as Schumacher quipped, 'a breakthrough a day keeps the crisis at bay'. This touching optimism is attributable to what may be called the Micawber Factor, in honour of Dickens's endearingly feckless character who believed that 'something will turn up'. Few, however, would suggest that Mr Micawber's wilfully extravagant and futile short-sightedness offered a model of sound economic living.

More prosaic economists, with less faith in the omnipotence of science, put their trust in something far more reliable – economics itself. These sober-minded individuals believe that there is no need to worry about conserving finite resources because all-powerful market forces will always intervene to save the world. The secret to saving the planet is to be found in something called the price mechanism and the theorems of competitive equilibrium. The typical response of this school is to argue as follows: As soon as a resource begins to run out, its supply relative to the demand for it will fall. Demand will exceed supply and its price will rise. The higher price will have two effects. First, there will be an added incentive to search for new supplies of the rare resource. Second, there will be extra incentives to develop a substitute. Of course, this assumes that there will always be new supplies to discover, or substitutes to develop. At this point, the prosaic school of thought is forced to call upon the same Micawber Factor on which their more optimistic colleagues are relying. Something will turn up – especially after the price mechanism has given scientists a helpful prod of encouragement.

There is, however, a slight snag. Some economists have seriously questioned whether the price mechanism can be relied upon to save the world from running out of exhaustible resources. In 1979 Partha Dasgupta, of the London School of Economics, and Geoffrey Heal, now of Columbia University, published a 500-page study entitled *Economic Theory and*

Exhaustible Resources.[2] Dasgupta and Heal concluded that fully informative price systems were an impossibility. Put simply, they were denying that any price mechanism could contain all the information necessary to predict or prevent a resource becoming exhausted. In fact they went even further, noting 'several reasons why the market is likely to provide incorrect incentives for exploration activity'. In short, the price mechanism was not only incapable of pointing in the right direction, it was likely to point in the wrong direction.

Bizarre as it may seem, Dasgupta and Heal reached their conclusions because their theoretical models allowed the future to exist. In contrast, the model of competitive equilibrium used by conventional economics assumes a timeless environment. People and companies all operate in a world in which the future does not exist and therefore neither does uncertainty. Once uncertainty is introduced into the theoretical framework, many of the results obtained from the standard model of competitive equilibrium are no longer valid. This is yet another example of the short-sightedness at the heart of economics which is having such a devastating effect throughout the world.

The Bland Leading the Blind

When one looks at the inadequacy of the price mechanism to deal with real and pressing problems it is difficult to conceive of economic theory as anything but shallow. Yet economists remain enthralled by the theories they espouse. As Schumacher remarked in *Small Is Beautiful*, it is a case of the bland leading the blind. Unfortunately, however, the blind are being entrusted with leading the world into the future – a future of which their central theories take no account. Is it any wonder, therefore, that they urge complacency in the face of the most pressing problems facing the planet?

Along with the three Theoretical Virtues of economic ortho-doxy – faith in market forces, hope that 'something will turn up' and love of economic growth – there are few dogmas more sacrosanct to conventional economics than that of free trade. Few conventional economists would dare question the belief that free trade is always good and that limits to trade are invariably bad. There are few indictments more damning to an economist than the accusation that he is advocating protectionism.

With this in mind, a heated exchange in March 1993 at a seminar held at the prestigious Ecole des Hautes Etudes Commerciales in France is of particular interest. On the first day of the seminar the five hundred students were addressed by Maurice Allais, a Nobel Prize-winner in economics. One can imagine the shock of the audience when Allais attacked the conventional maxim that free trade was in general beneficial. On the contrary, Allais argued, it could only be beneficial in certain exceptional circumstances. Denouncing the Maastricht Treaty, and by implication the European Union, Allais insisted that free trade could have favourable effects only when con-ducted between regions which were at comparable levels of economic development. He condemned vociferously 'the free trade policies of the European Commission'.

Allais' heresy could not go unanswered. Two days later Jacques Attali, president of the European Bank for Reconstruction and Development, reasserted orthodoxy. All anti-free-trade views were denounced as unequivocally '*stupides*', and Attali asserted that 'every obstacle to free trade is a factor which leads to recession'.

Commenting on this exchange of views, Paul Ormerod queried Attali's dogmatic assertion: 'It may, of course, be mere coincidence that at a time when barriers to trade within the

European Community are lower than ever before – indeed, the much publicized 1992 programme removing many trade restrictions has now come into force – Europe is entering not a boom, but a sharp recession!'

Nevertheless, and in spite of the dissident and sceptical voices of Allais and Ormerod, the vast majority of economists continue to repeat the mantra that 'free trade is always good, limits to trade are always bad'. Falling into line, William Hague declared his own belief in universal free trade on 17 September 1999 when he called for a transatlantic free trade area as part of a move towards global free trade by the year 2020. In this at least, the Conservative leader could rest assured that no voice would be raised in opposition. Tony Blair is equally in favour of global free trade. In such fundamentals Labour and Conservative share the same goal. Any argument between the party leaders would centre on whose policies were likely to achieve the goal more efficiently.

'Economically Correct'

Of course, there is also cross-party consensus on the other dogmas of conventional economics, particularly with regard to the Theoretical Virtues. Consequently there can be little surprise that politicians should compete with each other to be as 'economically correct' with regard to free trade as they are with regard to economic growth or market forces. After all, no ambitious politician wants to be accused of 'incorrectness'.

Global free trade has become an unquestionable moral dogma enshrined at the heart of modern economic theory. As such, politicians and economists are reluctant to question its presumptions and are failing to confront or even comprehend the effects of free trade on a world economy that is changing

45

radically. Yet with rapid technological innovation it is possible, even likely, that the globalization of trade will destabilize the industrialized world while at the same time exacerbating the problems facing the developing world.

The dogma of free trade has its roots in the nineteenth century and is based on the interrelated concepts of specialization and comparative advantage. Free trade theory stipulates that countries should specialize in those economic activities in which they excel in order to achieve a competitive edge, or a comparative advantage. They should abandon less efficient activities, relying on imports. These imports are paid for by exporting the surplus produced in the specialized industries. The result is greater efficiency and productivity and, therefore, higher levels of prosperity.

The rapid changes in the world over the past few decades throw the whole theory into question. New technology has made the global marketplace a practical, as opposed to a theoretical, reality. This has far-reaching consequences. During the past few years, four billion more people have entered the world economy. China, India, the countries of the Pacific rim and those of the former Soviet empire have all joined, or are trying to join, the Promised Land of global consumerism.

Sooner or later this is likely to cause major disruption. Labour costs in the developing world are as little as one-fiftieth of those in the developed, or over-developed, world. Since the free movement of technology and capital has 'levelled the playing field' the underpaid workers of the third world are now in direct competition with their comparatively rich counterparts in Europe and America. The workers of India, China and Bangladesh are part of the same global labour market as the workers of Britain and the United States. The implications are clear. Two identical enterprises, one in Britain and one in

Vietnam, produce an identical product, using identical technology, destined for identical markets. They both have access to the same pool of international capital. Indeed they are both part of the same multinational corporation. There is only one significant difference: labour costs in Vietnam are one-fiftieth of those in Britain. It is not necessary to be an economist to realize which enterprise has the comparative advantage.

In developed countries, the cost to an average manufacturing company of paying its workforce is an amount equal to between 25 and 30 per cent of sales. Thus, if an average company decides to maintain only its head office and sales force in its home country, while transferring production to the developing world, it will save about 20 per cent of sales volume. This will mean that a company with sales of £500 million will increase its pre-tax profits by up to £100 million a year. Indeed, free trade will leave the company with little choice but to take this course of action. If it decides – through patriotism, a social conscience, genuine concern for the future of its workforce, or whatever other reason – to resist the low-cost option it will be unable to compete with the cheap imports of its less scrupulous rivals. The choice is a stark one – uproot or perish.

It could of course be argued that this is merely a fair redistribution of wealth to the poorer parts of the world – though it is difficult to see such a line of argument winning much sympathy with electorates or trade union representatives in over-developed countries. In practice, however, relocation in the third world enriches the multinational corporations without bestowing a great deal of extra wealth on third world populations. (The impact of globalization on the developing world is discussed at greater length in chapters 14 and 15.)

Resorting to the Micawber Factor, economists will point out that the loss of manufacturing jobs will be replaced by jobs in the service sector or in new high-tech industries. Here is free trade theory in practice, they would argue. Since comparative advantage in manufactures has moved to the developing world, the developed world should specialize in the service economy and new technology. But this is short-sighted. In the near future new technology will also make it far easier to transfer the service sector to the developing countries. Video-satellite links make it possible already to hold board meetings between members who are physically in different parts of the world. Microchip technology means that finance capital can be switched anywhere in the world in a fraction of a second. Why should financial institutions maintain expensive tower blocks in London, New York or Paris when they could set up far more cheaply in a dozen or more developing cities? Why should they pay white-collar salaries in Europe or America when office workers in the third world can be trained to do the same work for a fraction of the money? Several major companies – Swissair for example – have already relocated significant parts of their accounts departments to India. In the emerging global market the comparative advantage for high-tech industries and services, as well as for manufactures, resides in the third world.

It goes without saying that some sections of the service sector, such as health and education, could not be transferred overseas. Yet these are not the areas of the economy that produce wealth, but the areas that dispense it. Despite the fact that health and education are included in GNP, it is not possible to lose the part of the economy that produces wealth and expect to be able to maintain the part that dispenses it. You can't spend what you haven't earned.

Spending What We Haven't Earned

And this brings us to the most popular aspect of free trade as far as the public at large is concerned – the availability of cheap imports. As society in the developed world is increasingly consumer-driven, the ability to buy certain products more cheaply because they have been produced in low-cost countries appears to be the greatest argument for the desirability of free trade. This, however, is merely another case of spending what we haven't earned, at least in the longer term. Many consumers, lured by the easy availability of credit, are already spending what they haven't earned in the sense of living on borrowed money. Yet even if they are not living on borrowed money, consumers in the over-developed world may be living on borrowed time. Ultimately, the real cost to consumers of cheaper goods is that many may lose their jobs, most will get paid less, and all will be taxed more to cover the cost of increased unemployment and the multifarious social problems that go with it. If four billion extra people enter the same world market for labour at a fraction of the price paid to those in the over-developed world, it doesn't take an economist to see that the hidden surcharge on cheap imported goods is still to be paid.

So much for the potential losers, but who are the winners in the onward rush towards global free trade? The immediate winners are the multinational corporations, which can benefit from a seemingly inexhaustible supply of cheap labour. These corporations can switch production to whatever part of the world offers the lowest labour costs, a fact that ensures downward pressure on wage levels in the developing world as each developing economy competes with the others for foreign investment. It is scarcely surprising, therefore, that the greatest champions of free trade are those who gain most from it, i.e.

the multinationals. The globalization of the market is crucial to them, both in order to produce cheaply and to sell universally. Their combined power is enormous. They account for one-third of global output and one-third of all foreign direct investment. This power is being wielded to ensure that nothing stands in the way of global free trade.

Few would argue that multinationals are the greatest beneficiaries of free trade, but surely others are benefiting also. Aren't ordinary people in the developing countries benefiting from the massive levels of foreign investment? To a degree certainly, at least in material terms, but the vast majority of the investment never finds itself in the pockets, or the mouths, of ordinary people. In most developing countries a small handful of people control the overwhelming majority of the nation's resources. It is this privileged few who benefit, assisting the multinationals to assemble the cheap labour used to manufacture products for the developed world. At most, the ordinary people receive the meagre scraps from the multinational table. In fact, however, even the meagre material benefits are wiped out by the massive disruption that globalization is causing to third world economies and societies. (See chapter 14.)

Armed with the Theoretical Virtues, conventional economists will dismiss all these arguments. Nothing can shake their faith in the 'hidden hand' of market forces or their passionate love affair with economic growth. Those non-believers who insist on erecting doomsday scenarios can be ignored as neo-Luddites trying to hold back the inevitable tide of progress. For economists the future is bright. Eventually global free trade will enrich the whole world so that all can enjoy the benefits of material wealth and consumer society. They dream of everyone in the world, all six billion (and counting), becoming global consumers in a global market. Six billion cars, six billion

CD players, six billion personal computers, six billion mobile phones...

Earlier, it was suggested that economists are people who know how to count but have forgotten how to see. Perhaps, however, they have also forgotten how to count. At the beginning of this chapter it was mentioned that in 1973 America consumed approximately 40 per cent of the world's non-renewable resources in spite of containing only 5.6 per cent of the world's population. By 1993, the 5 per cent of the world's population living in America were still responsible for 24 per cent of the world's energy consumption and nearly 30 per cent of the world's materials consumption.[3] What happens when global free trade transforms the other 95 per cent of the world into happy consumers? The answer, if the rest of the world prove to be as good consumers as the Americans, is that they will require 674 per cent of the world's finite resources, nearly seven times more than are actually known to exist. And this doesn't even take account of the added pollution that those billions of extra consumers will produce. Under such circumstances we will certainly have a world of global consumers, but not in the sense intended by the economists. The globe itself, or life on it, will be consumed.

1 C. Dernbach, 'In Focus: WTO and Sustainable Development', published as part of 'Foreign Policy In Focus', a joint project of the Interhemispheric Resource Center and the Institute for Policy Studies: www.foreignpolicy-infocus.org.

2 Partha Dasgupta and Geoffrey Heal, *Economic Theory and Exhaustible Resources*, Cambridge: Cambridge University Press, 1979.

3 C. Dernbach, 'In Focus: WTO and Sustainable Development'.

5

Mechanistic and Materialistic

The attempt to describe and eventually to control the economic activities of human beings by means of economic models necessarily requires a ruthless and extreme simplification of the picture of man. Man is seen either as a mechanical robot, whose reactions are ascertainable and predictable like those of mindless matter, or as a 'rational' homo oeconomicus solely concerned with material self-enrichment. Neither of these two pictures bears the marks of humanity. An economic teaching built on such a basis cannot possibly be helpful in solving the economic problems now oppressing us... [1]

E.F. Schumacher

Almost thirty years ago Professor Phelps Brown, in his presidential address to the Royal Economic Society, talked about 'The Underdevelopment of Economics'. He complained about 'the smallness of the contribution' made by the most conspicuous developments of economics to the solution of pressing problems such as inflation, environmental protection, overseas development, urbanization, and the quality of life.

Schumacher believed that the preoccupation of economists with logical, mathematical and econometric subtleties had led to the almost total neglect of crucial determining factors. If economics was to play any meaningful part in solving the most pressing problems facing humanity and the planet it would have to look beyond the purely economic to the wider questions of life which gave economics its purpose. In other words, to become truly relevant, economics must look beyond itself: the 'how' of economics had to be reconciled with the 'why' of human existence. Economics needed to become meta-economics. Nowhere has this bedrock reality been discussed more lucidly and potently than in Schumacher's *Small Is Beautiful*. This chapter and the next therefore follow Schumacher very closely, employing his arguments and often his own words, either paraphrased or verbatim.

Schumacher divided meta-economics into three distinct areas. In the first place, economics needed a metaphysical critique of itself, an examination of its intrinsic purpose. Secondly, there was a need on the part of economics to recognize that the physical factors of life are essentially qualitative as well as quantitative. Finally, economics needed to study man in his wholeness and not consider him only as 'economic man', since *homo oeconomicus* was an abstraction devoid of essential humanity.

The fundamental error of modern economics is its mechanistic approach. It has evolved ever more intransigently in a merely quantitative direction, erecting econometric models based on mathematical theory which assume that the actions of people are essentially the same as the behaviour of atoms. Yet are the 'facts' of economics in their essential nature the same as the facts of mathematics or physics? Are human beings, the *dramatis personae* of economics, similar to atoms in their essential nature? If so, does this not strip humanity of its freedom, its responsibility, its creativeness, its purpose, its meaning? In essence, does it not strip humanity of its humanity? For Schumacher, such questions were at the heart of meta-economics: 'If economists continue to refuse to face such fundamental metaphysical – or, if you prefer the term, philosophical – questions, I cannot see that they can have any idea of what they are really teaching and what is the relationship of their teaching to truth.'[2]

Price Versus Value

Failure to address metaphysical questions has led to many of the central errors of conventional economics. The preoccupation with the physical as opposed to the metaphysical, the quantitative as opposed to the qualitative, has many practical ramifications. For example, the economic obsession with the quantitative has led to price eclipsing value, since price is quantitative whereas value is qualitative. Price is measurable mechanically whereas value can only be evaluated by making value judgements based on philosophical concepts. Since conventional economics shuns these meta-economic concepts, it speaks of 'value' only in terms of the market – and 'market value' is merely another way of saying 'price'. Therefore, intrinsic value does not exist for conventional economics.

The consequences of this lack of distinction between price and value are far-reaching. As discussed in previous chapters, it has led to a failure to differentiate between primary and secondary goods, or between renewable and non-renewable goods. It has led to the purely quantitative pricing of the economy in terms of gross national product, 'which adds everything together, whether it is good or bad, healthy or unhealthy, life-sustaining or life-destroying'.[3]

Similarly, it has fuelled the idea of the 'free market'. Since the market is measured only in terms of price it is assumed that the consumer makes only price-induced judgements. In theory at least, the ideal consumer is a bargain-hunter who is concerned with nothing but price. Consumers do not care whether the goods they are buying are home produced or imported, renewable or non-renewable, organic or chemical, natural or genetically modified, cruelly or humanely produced. Consumers who make any of these value judgements prior to making a purchase are not behaving according to the econometric price mechanism that governs economic theory. They are not behaving as *homo oeconomicus* should. They have stepped out of line by bringing into the equation value as opposed to price, quality as opposed to quantity, and metaphysics as opposed to physics. They are behaving not as predictable atoms, but as free-willed human beings. By exercising free will, people throw a spanner into the economic works.

Clearly, if it is to address the real issues and redress the errors of its past, economics needs to find a meta-economic dimension. That is, it needs to go beyond mathematical theory to metaphysical reality. It needs to recognize that people matter *in themselves* and are not merely units of production and consumption. It needs to acknowledge the eternally radical statement that 'Man shall not live by bread alone…' and to recognize that life is not just a science but an art. In short, if economics is to have any useful or meaningful role, it needs to have a meta-economic 'soul'.

The absence of 'soul' in economics is itself only a result and a reflection of the growth of philosophical humanism. Quite simply, humanism took the soul out of human affairs by assuming that human beings did not have souls. The evolution of the concept of soullessness was discussed by the economic historian R.H. Tawney:

From a spiritual being who, in order to survive, must devote a reasonable attention to economic interests, man seems sometimes to have become an economic animal, who will be prudent, nevertheless, if he takes due precaution to assure his spiritual well-being.

The result is an attitude which forms so fundamental a part of modern political thought, that both its precarious philosophical basis and the contrast which it offers with the conceptions of earlier generations are commonly forgotten. Its essence is a dualism which regards the secular and the religious aspects of life ... as parallel and independent provinces, governed by different laws, judged by different standards, and amenable to different authorities. To the most representative minds of the Reformation as of the Middle Ages, a philosophy which treated the transactions of commerce and the institutions of society as indifferent to religion would have appeared, not merely morally reprehensible, but intellectually absurd.[4]

'Get Rich, Be Happy'

One evident result of this development is the contemporary belief that all humanity's problems can be solved by the attainment of universal material prosperity. The road to riches is the road to happiness. This dominant modern belief is irresistibly alluring because it suggests that the faster you get one desirable thing the more surely do you attain another. It has the added attraction of being devoid of any ethical constraints, such as the need for self-sacrifice. On the contrary, the more we try to selfishly enrich ourselves the happier we shall be. The materialist mantra is 'Get Rich, Be Happy'. Once this golden rule is accepted the only problem confronting humanity is an economic and technological one: how do we make everybody richer so that everybody can be happier?

Gandhi spoke disparagingly about 'dreaming of systems so perfect that no one will need to be good'. Yet the golden rule cited above doesn't mention being good, for that is irrelevant. On the contrary, if goodness is an obstacle to happiness it is to be shunned. The name of the game is self-gratification, not self-sacrifice. 'For at least another hundred years,' wrote John Maynard Keynes, 'we must pretend to ourselves and to every one that fair is foul and foul is fair, for foul is useful and fair is not. Avarice and usury and precaution must be our gods for a little longer still. For only they can lead us out of the tunnel of economic necessity into daylight.'[5] Keynes justified such an unethical approach on the grounds that it was necessary so that everyone could become rich. Once people were rich, he reasoned, they would 'once more value ends above means and prefer the good to the useful'. In the meantime, ethical considerations were an actual hindrance to be avoided. For Keynes, as Schumacher suggested, 'the road to heaven is paved with bad intentions'.

The three steps to this materialist heaven espoused by Keynes are, first, a belief that universal prosperity is possible; second, that it is achievable on the basis of the materialist philosophy of 'enrich yourself'; and third, that it will lead to happiness.

There is an obvious problem attached to Keynes's line of reasoning. At what point will people decide that they are rich enough to be happy, or that they are rich enough to want to start being good? Indeed, what exactly is 'enough'? Conventional economics, obsessed with perpetual growth, has no concept of 'enough'. On the contrary, the key word in economics is not 'enough' but 'more'. And although there are poor societies that have too little, there are no rich societies saying that they have enough, still less that they have too much.

This prompts another question: Can a society be called 'happy', however materially affluent, if it always wants more? Clearly, the answer is 'no'. It is not satisfied, a word whose root in Latin, *satis*, means 'enough'. It can be seen, therefore, that the 'Get Rich, Be Happy' mantra is a futile hymn to a false god. It is neither satisfying in practice nor satisfactory in principle. In fact, a more appropriate hymn for the restlessly rich countries of the world would be the Rolling Stones anthem, 'I Can't Get No Satisfaction'.

Need Versus Greed

Conventional economists such as Keynes make the same perennially fatal mistake whenever they choose to ignore the metaphysical truths that underpin physical facts. They forget that, at least in part, need is physical whereas greed is metaphysical. As such, need is limited but greed is unlimited. It is larger than the world and may, if unchecked, destroy our planet. As Gandhi said, 'Earth provides enough to satisfy every man's need, but not every man's greed'. Such metaphysical realities require a philosophical approach to economics.

If it is to survive, humanity must rediscover its higher calling. We must rise above being merely *homo oeconomicus* to become once more what we claim to be, *homo sapiens*. At this point it should be recalled that *sapiens* does not mean modern, but wise. Our species is capable of wisdom even if we all too often fail to attain it. Perhaps it may also be timely to emphasize, though this is not the place to discuss the issue at greater length, that wisdom is not merely knowledge or understanding, and still less is it mere intelligence. It is the application of experience, knowledge and understanding in a way that both apprehends and serves objective truth. This is the challenge facing humanity.

Schumacher wrote that man has become too clever to be able to survive without wisdom. As humanity proceeds into the third millennium, the need for wisdom is greater than ever. Through the application of new technology, man is now capable of consuming the planet at an ever-increasing speed. Without wisdom modern man is like a child with a machine gun, both naively ignorant and physically dangerous. Cleverness without wisdom is perilous, and man cannot afford the luxury of the one without the security and guidance of the other.

Seen in this context, the Keynesian view is the antithesis of wisdom because the cultivation of greed and envy must be ultimately destructive. As Schumacher observed, 'The hope that the pursuit of goodness and virtue can be postponed until we have attained universal prosperity and that by the single-minded pursuit of wealth, without bothering our heads about spiritual and moral questions, we could establish peace on earth, is an unrealistic, unscientific, and irrational hope.'[6]

From an economic point of view, the wise approach centres on the concept of permanence or sustainability. It is clear that continued and unlimited growth is not sustainable. The very suggestion that there can be infinite growth in a finite space with finite resources is an obvious absurdity. Yet there can be no reduction in growth and no sustainable future for as long as the distinction between need and desire is deliberately blurred. The cultivation of desire and the creation of needless wants is at the core of the economic dilemma facing the modern world. Every increase in desire increases one's perceived dependence on outside forces over which one cannot have control, and this in turn contributes towards a general insecurity and restlessness. One who desires is, by definition, unsatisfied.

Only by a reduction in desire can there be any reduction in the general restlessness of humanity and, in consequence, a reduction on the demands we place on the planet. As the Colombian economist Joaquin Moreno observed, 'Gain moves human beings to attain their goals, but ultimately without a purpose that transcends consumption all we have to gain is our reduction as human beings.'[7] The same point was put poignantly by Alexander Solzhenitsyn: 'Man has set for himself the goal of conquering the world but in the process loses his soul.'[8]

Solzhenitsyn's words are, of course, a variation on the words of Jesus Christ: 'For what is a man profited, if he shall gain the whole world, and lose his own soul?'[9] Such is the folly of economic man that he is not even leaving himself a choice. He is set to lose his soul *and* the world, poisoning the one with greed and the other with the pillage and pollution it causes.

1 E.F. Schumacher, 'Does Economics Help? An Exploration of Meta-Economics' in Joan Robinson (ed.), *After Keynes*, Oxford: Basil Blackwell, 1973, p. 36.

2 Ibid., p. 34.

3 Ibid.

4 Quoted in Schumacher, 'Does Economics Help?', p. 35.

5 Schumacher, *Small Is Beautiful*, p. 19.

6 Ibid., p. 26.

7 Joaquin Moreno, unpublished essay presented to the Phoenix Institute Summer Programme at Brasenose College, Oxford in August 1999.

8 Alexander Solzhenitsyn, interview with Joseph Pearce, Moscow, 20 July 1998.

9 Matthew 16:26.

6

Economics with Soul

The wound of our individualistic and materialistic society will not be healed, the deep chasm will not be bridged, by no matter what system, if the system itself is materialistic in principle and mechanical in practice.[1]

Pius XII

That economics is inherently subservient to philosophy is implicit from the previous chapter. Economics is a derivative, i.e. it is inherently subservient to, and dependent upon, philosophy. The errors of conventional economics spring from the humanism of the late Renaissance and the Enlightenment. The philosophical assumption that man has invented God, rather than that God has created man, means that humanity has placed itself at the centre of creation. With the rise of humanism, humankind became the measure of all things, the test of truth and falsehood. It was a short step from this assumption to its logical conclusion, that all truth was subjective. There was no such thing as Truth, merely individual truths held by individuals. This led inevitably to the belief that no truth is valid except my own. More recently, this has evolved into the postmodernist assumption that there is no truth at all, not even my own. All so-called truths are merely subjective beliefs with no objective authority. Indeed, there is no such thing as objective authority, only subjective opinion.

This philosophical fragmentation is the father of conventional economics. Since the individual is all that matters, individualism becomes the *raison d'être* of economic affairs. And since there is no objective authority, individuals are free to do their 'own thing'. They are unhampered in their actions or their desires by ethical considerations since ethics, like everything else, are a matter of personal choice. The deification of the self, uninhibited by any code of morality, has led inevitably to the triumph of selfishness. The me-myself-I mentality seeks nothing but self-gratification. Greed becomes virtue.

If, however, economics is derivative and accepts its instructions, consciously or otherwise, from philosophy, it follows that the nature of economics will change when the instructions change. It is, therefore, instructive to explore the ways in which concepts of 'economic' and 'uneconomic' alter when the assumptions of philosophical humanism or materialism are replaced by the teachings of any of the major world religions. For example, it is axiomatic that human labour is one of the fundamental factors of production yet conventional economics sees it very differently from the way it is perceived by, say, Buddhism or Christianity.

As Schumacher emphasized, the conventional economist has been trained to view labour or work as little more than a necessary evil. To the employer it is merely an item of cost, to be minimized even if it can't be eliminated altogether by automation. To the employee it is a 'disutility'; to work is to be forced to suspend one's leisure or comfort for something less pleasurable, and wages are the compensation received for the inconvenience. From the point of view of the employer the ideal is to have output without employees, while from the point of view of the employee the ideal is to have income without employment.

The consequences of such a view of labour are far-reaching. If the ideal with regard to work is to get rid of it, every measure that reduces the workload is a good thing. Apart from the automation made possible by new technology, the traditional method of reducing the workload has been through the 'division of labour'. This is not ordinary specialization, which humanity has practised from time immemorial, but the division of the production process into the minutest parts so that each part, more often than not, is both unskilled and uninteresting for the labourer practising it. This, in turn, alienates labourers from their work still further, accentuating the view that work is a necessary evil.

Labour's Threefold Purpose

For the Christian or the Buddhist, labour is viewed very differently. As Schumacher stipulated, it has at least a threefold purpose. It gives individuals the opportunity 'to utilize and develop [their] faculties'; it enables them to overcome their selfishness by joining with others in a common task; and it brings forth the goods and services 'needed for a becoming existence'. Specifically, the teaching of the Second Vatican Council states that labour 'constitutes a road to holiness' through the opportunities it offers in four distinct areas: self-improvement through the development of the human personality by the exercising of its qualities and potentialities; the ability to help our fellow citizens through the social dimension of labour ('labour is not a self-centred activity but an altruistic one; we do not work exclusively for ourselves, but for others too'); the improvement of society at large and the Creation; and the opportunity to imitate Christ in works of active charity.[2]

Such a view has many consequences. The excessive division of labour becomes an unacceptable evil because it strips labour of its virtue and its dignity, rendering it 'meaningless, boring and stultifying'. To sacrifice the dignity of labour in order to increase output would indicate a greater concern with goods than with people. Any employer seeking to do so would betray an evil lack of compassion and a soul-destroying degree of attachment to the primitive aspects of this worldly existence. Equally, the pursuit of leisure to the detriment or exclusion of work would be considered a negation of one of the basic truths of a good life, 'namely that work and leisure are complementary' and inseparable. The joys of work and leisure are parts of a virtuous day, lived to the full.

To the Buddhist and the Christian, automation has its limits. The purpose of technology is neither to minimize labour nor to maximize profits. It is to serve and preserve the dignity and well-being of humanity. Technology must be the servant of man, not man the servant of technology. According to the Buddhist economist Ananda Coomaraswamy, it is important to distinguish between the appropriate and the inappropriate use of technology: 'The craftsman himself, can always, if allowed to, draw the delicate distinction between the machine and the tool. The carpet loom is a tool, a contrivance for holding warp threads at a stretch for the pile to be woven round them by the craftsmen's fingers; but the power loom is a machine, and its significance as a destroyer of culture lies in the fact that it does the essentially human part of the work.'[3]

'Human Society Is Not a Machine'

This view was echoed in more general terms by Pope Pius XII when he expressed concern that technology was stripping human society of its humanity: 'Human society is not a machine, and must not be made such, not even in the economic field…'[4] Elsewhere, Pope Pius condemned the way in which materialistic society, conceptualized as a machine, attempts to quantify the qualitative and mechanize the organic: 'modern society, which wishes to plan and organize all things, comes into conflict, since it is conceived as a machine, with that which is living, and which therefore cannot be subjected to quantitative calculations…'[5] Pius's predecessor, Pope Pius XI, was even more forthright in his condemnation of the dehumanizing impact of automation and the excessive division of labour: 'And so bodily labour, which … was decreed by Providence for the good of man's body and soul, is in many instances changed into an instrument of perversion; for from the factory dead matter goes out improved, whereas men there are corrupted and degraded.'[6]

The belief that labour is good for man's body and soul is radically at odds with the concept that it is merely a production cost or a necessary but regrettable disutility. Expressing the former view, the Indian philosopher and economist J.C. Kumarappa summed the matter up as follows:

> If the nature of the work is properly appreciated and applied, it will stand in the same relation to the higher faculties as food is to the physical body. It nourishes and enlivens the higher man and urges him to produce the best he is capable of. It directs his free will along the proper course and disciplines the animal in him into progressive channels. It furnishes an excellent

background for man to display his scale of values and develop his personality.[7]

Conversely, when the nature of work is improperly appreciated and applied, as, for instance, on an automated assembly line in a modern factory, it is often soul diminishing instead of soul enhancing. It degrades and does not dignify the labourer. This is the end result of an economic system which treats labour with relative contempt. Conventional economists regard goods as the end for which economic activity is carried out and labour merely as a means to that end. In the production process, the goods are more important than the people. It is only as consumers that people attain any worthwhile status because consumption is considered more important than creative activity. Thus emphasis is shifted from the worker to the product of work, from the human to the sub-human. This, for the Christian or the Buddhist, is standing truth on its head. It is a surrender to evil.

A similar difference of approach can be seen with regard to consumption itself. Schumacher criticized the way that conventional economists measure the 'standard of living' by the amount of consumption. It is assumed that an individual who consumes more is 'better off' than one who consumes less. In order to feel that we are 'well off', we must consume at least as much as our neighbour, preferably more. Keeping up with the Joneses is the measure of a person's success. It is little surprise, therefore, that we are seen increasingly as consumers rather than as human beings. Modern society is 'consumer-driven'. We are not people, still less people with souls. We are consumers, mere economic functionaries, serving economic growth.

Higher Reality

Such a view is anathema to Buddhist or Christian teaching. For the Buddhist or the Christian, the purpose of life is to conform one's actions and desires to the higher reality governing the cosmos. To be truly contented, to be at peace with oneself, it is essential to be at peace with both Creation and its Creator. It follows inexorably from this principal assumption that all economic activity is merely a means to that ultimate end. Clearly one is not at peace if one is constantly trying to out-consume one's neighbour. The Christian or Buddhist wants only enough; the consumer always wants more. The former is limited by need, the latter unlimited by greed. The former seeks sustainable sufficiency, the latter unending growth.

Perhaps the crucial difference between conventional economics and the teaching of Buddhism or Christianity is their respective approach to the natural environment. Since the humanist philosophy that instructs modern economics is, quite literally, self-centred, its essential selfishness has led to a fatal disregard of the world around it. This environmentally unfriendly approach was discussed by the French political philosopher Bertrand de Jouvenal, who characterized 'western man' in terms which, according to Schumacher, 'may be taken as a fair description of the modern economist':

He tends to count nothing as an expenditure, other than human effort; he does not seem to mind how much mineral matter he wastes and, far worse, how much living matter he destroys. He does not seem to realize at all that human life is a dependent part of an ecosystem of many different forms of life. As the world is ruled from towns where men are cut off from any form of life other than human, the feeling of belonging to

an ecosystem is not revived. This results in a harsh and improv-
ident treatment of things upon which we ultimately depend,
such as water and trees.[8]

Schumacher compared the approach of 'western man' to the
teaching of the Buddha 'who enjoins a reverent and non-
violent attitude' to all sentient beings and also, 'with great
emphasis, to trees'. According to Buddhist teaching, every
follower of the Buddha 'ought to plant a tree every few years
and look after it until it is safely established'. Similarly,
Christianity teaches that man is the steward of Creation. He has
the duty, bestowed on him by God, to care for that which God
has created. This teaching was expounded with succinct clarity
by Pope John Paul II on 30 December 1987:

Nor can the moral character of development exclude respect
for the beings which constitute *the natural world, which the*
ancient Greeks – alluding precisely to the order *which distin-*
guishes it – called the 'cosmos'. Such realities also demand
respect, by virtue of a threefold consideration which it is useful
to reflect upon carefully.

The first consideration *is the appropriateness of acquiring*
a growing awareness *of the fact that one cannot use with*
impunity the different categories of beings, whether living or
inanimate – animals, plants, the natural elements – simply as
one wishes, according to one's own economic needs. On the
contrary, one must take into account the nature of each being
and of its mutual connection *in an ordered system, which is*
precisely the 'cosmos'.

The second consideration *is based on the realization –*
which is perhaps more urgent – that natural resources are
limited; *some are not, as it is said,* renewable. *Using them as if*

they were inexhaustible, with absolute dominion, *seriously endangers their availability not only for the present generation but above all for generations to come.*

The third consideration *refers directly to the consequences of a certain type of development on the* quality of life *in the industrialized zones. We all know that the direct or indirect result of industrialization is, ever more frequently, the pollution of the environment, with serious consequences for the health of the population.*

Once again it is evident that development, the planning which governs it, and the way in which resources are used must include respect for moral demands. One of the latter undoubtedly imposes limits on the use of the natural world. The dominion granted to man by the Creator is not an absolute power, nor can one speak of a freedom to 'use and misuse', or to dispose of things as one pleases. The limitation imposed from the beginning by the Creator himself and expressed symbolically by the prohibition not to 'eat of the fruit of the tree' (cf. Genesis 2:16–17) shows clearly enough that, when it comes to the natural world, we are subject not only to biological laws but also to moral ones, which cannot be violated with impunity.

A true concept of development cannot ignore the use of the elements of nature, the renewability of resources and the consequences of haphazard industrialization – three considerations which alert our consciences to the moral dimension of development.[9]

Nature-reverence

Perhaps the best-known example of nature-reverence in Christian tradition is St Francis of Assisi's 'Canticle of Brother Sun':

Be praised, my Lord, in all your creatures,
especially Brother Sun
who makes daytime,
and through him you give us light.
And he is beautiful, radiant with great splendour,
and he is a sign
that tells, All-highest, of you.

Be praised, my Lord, for Sister Moon and the stars;
you formed them in the sky,
bright and precious and beautiful.

Be praised, my Lord, for Brother Wind,
and for the air and the clouds,
and for fair, and every kind of weather,
by which you give your creatures food.

Be praised, my Lord, for Sister Water,
who is most useful and humble
and lovely and chaste.

Be praised, my Lord, for Brother Fire,
through whom you light up the night for us;
and he is beautiful and jolly
and lusty and strong.

Be praised, my Lord, for our Sister Mother Earth,
who keeps us, and feeds us,
and brings forth fruits of many kinds,
with coloured flowers and plants as well.

There is a remarkable similarity between the Franciscan spirit of this poem and the words of a letter attributed to the American Indian chief Seattle. The letter is believed to have been sent in 1854 to President Franklin Pierce, following the request of the US government to acquire the tribal lands of the chief's people. Although the historical authenticity of the letter has been questioned, Chief Seattle's words are particularly poignant because they not only praise nature but protest at its wanton destruction. They also illustrate potently the extent to which concepts of 'economic' and 'uneconomic' are governed by philosophical precepts:

How can you buy or sell the sky, the warmth of the land? The idea is strange to us. If we do not own the freshness of the air and the sparkle of the water, how can you buy them? Every part of this earth is sacred to my people. Every shining pine needle, every sandy shore, every mist in the dark woods, every clearing and humming insect is holy in the memory and experience of my people. The sap which courses through the trees carries the memories of the red man.

The white man's dead forget the country of their birth when they go to walk among the stars. Our dead never forget this beautiful earth, for it is the mother of the red man. We are part of the earth and it is part of us. The perfumed flowers are our sisters; the deer, the horse, the great eagle, these are our brothers. The rocky crests, the juices in the meadows, the body heat of the pony, and man – all belong to the same family ... This shining water that moves in the streams and rivers is not just water but the blood of our ancestors ... The rivers are our brothers, they quench our thirst ...

We know that the white man does not understand our ways. One portion of land is the same to him as the next, for he is a stranger who comes in the night and takes from the land whatever he needs. The earth is not his brother but his enemy, and when he has conquered it, he moves on. He leaves his father's graves behind, and he does not care ... His father's grave and his children's birthright are forgotten. He treats his mother, the earth, and his brother, the sky, as things to be bought, plundered, sold like sheep or bright beads. His appetite will devour the earth and leave behind only a desert...

What is man without the beasts? If all the beasts were gone, man would die from a great loneliness of spirit. For whatever happens to the beasts, soon happens to man. All things are connected ... Whatever befalls the earth befalls the sons of the earth ... Man did not weave the web of life: he is merely a strand in it. Whatever he does to the web, he does to himself.

Whether the perspective is that of a Buddhist, a Christian or a pantheist there is unity in the belief that economics must have 'soul'. Without it, both humanity and the planet are placed in peril. The consequences for humanity of continued existence within a soulless economy were encapsulated in rhetorically robust prose by Wendell Berry in his 1977 book *The Unsettling of America*:

An American is probably the most unhappy citizen in the history of the world ... From morning to night, he does not touch anything he has produced himself, in which he can take pride. For all his leisure and recreation, he feels bad, he looks bad, he is overweight, his health is poor. His air, water and food are all known to contain poisons ... He suspects that his love life is not as fulfilling as other people's. He wishes that he had been born sooner, or later. He does not know why his children are the way they are. He does not understand what they say. He does not care much and does not know why he does not care. He does not know what his wife wants or what he wants. Certain advertisements and pictures in magazines make him suspect that he is basically unattractive … He does not know what he would do if he lost his job, if the economy failed … if his wife left him, if his children ran away, if he should be found to be incurably ill. And for these anxieties, of course, he consults certified experts who, in turn, consult certified experts about their anxieties.

For all their dark comedy, these words are deeply tragic. They expose the real absence at the heart of modern society. The absence of a heart itself.

Humanity, at the mercy of an economy that has lost itself in a maelstrom of its own making, has lapsed into a state of fatalistic apathy. Yet we are not powerless to act. We have power through the free will we possess. The world in which we find ourselves has lurched towards crisis point. Having blundered our way into the mess, we have a duty to find our way out. Our future, and the future of the world we live in, depends on it.

1 Address to the International Union of Catholic Women's Leagues, 14 April 1939; quoted in Robert C. Pollock (ed.) *The Mind of Pius XII*, London: W. Foulsham & Co. Ltd, 1955, p. 33.

2 John Paul II, *Agenda for the Third Millennium*, London: HarperCollins/Fount, 1996, pp. 156–7.

3 Quoted in Schumacher, *Small Is Beautiful*, p. 46.

4 Robert C. Pollock (ed.), *The Mind of Pius XII*, London: W. Foulsham & Co. Ltd, 1955, p. 46.

5 Ibid., pp. 46–7.

6 Pius XI, *Quadragesimo Anno*, London: Catholic Truth Society, 1963, p. 53.

7 Quoted in Schumacher, *Small Is Beautiful*, p. 46.

8 Quoted in Schumacher, *Small Is Beautiful*, p. 49.

9 John Paul II, *Sollicitudo Rei Socialis*, London: Catholic Truth Society, 1988, pp. 64–6.

PART 3

Size Matters

7

The Cult of Bigness

I hold the old mystical dogma that what Man has done, Man can do. My critics seem to hold a still more mystical dogma: that Man cannot possibly do a thing because he has done it. That is what seems to be meant by saying that small property is 'antiquated'. It really means that all property is dead. There is nothing to be reached upon the present lines except the increasing loss of property by everybody, as something swallowed up into a system equally impersonal and inhuman...

There is nothing in front but a flat wilderness of standardization ... But it is strange that some of us should have seen sanity, if only in a vision, while the rest go forward chained eternally to enlargement without liberty and progress without hope.[1]

G.K. Chesterton

Macrophilia – the cult of bigness – has been the prevailing trend in economic thinking for almost two hundred years. It is rooted in the theory of 'economies of scale' which, alongside the 'hidden hand' of market forces and the dogma of economic growth, is a cornerstone of conventional economics. Such was its power in the early part of the twentieth century that the two 'extremes' of economic theory – capitalism and communism – were united in its praise. Both systems assumed that big was best.

In capitalist systems, the belief in 'economies of scale' found expression in the clamour for mergers and acquisitions that resulted in the establishment of huge multinational corporations. By 1960 the fifty largest industrial corporations in the United States employed an average of 80,000 workers each. General Motors employed 595,000 and Vail's AT&T employed 736,000. This meant, with an average household size of 3.3, that more than four million people were dependent on these two companies alone. In France, in 1963, fourteen hundred firms – a mere 0.25 per cent of all companies – employed 38 per cent of the work force.[2] Government policy in Germany, Britain and many other countries actively encouraged mergers to create even larger companies, in the belief that the resulting economies of scale would enable them to compete more efficiently with the American giants.

Meanwhile, communists were as addicted to macrophilia as were their capitalist counterparts. Marx had associated the 'increasing scale of industrial establishments' with the 'wider development of their material powers'. Lenin concurred, arguing that 'huge enterprises, trusts and syndicates had brought the mass production technique to its highest level of development'. Putting his theory into practice, Lenin set about transforming the post-revolution Soviet economy on the lines of big is best. His ideal was simple. Economic life should be organized into the smallest possible number of the largest possible units. Following Lenin's death his successor, Josef Stalin, carried on in the same vein. Vast new steel complexes were built at Magnitogorsk and Zaporozhtal, a copper smelting plant was constructed at Balkhash, and tractor plants at Kharkov and Stalingrad. Stalin's economic outlook was as simple as his predecessor's. He would find out how large a given American installation was, then order construction of an even larger one.

The Cult of Bigness

In *The Cult of Bigness in Soviet Economic Planning*, Dr Leon M. Herman wrote that throughout the USSR local politicians became involved in a race to attract the 'world's largest projects'. By 1938 the Communist Party was warning of 'gigantomania' but it was too late to reverse the process. According to Herman, communist leaders throughout the eastern bloc remained victims of 'the addiction to bigness'. In the early 1980s the Soviets completed the construction of the world's largest lorry-manufacturing installation. It required a whole new city of 160,000 people with a complex of plants and conveyors extending over forty square miles, an area nearly twice the size of Manhattan Island in New York.[3]

Such faith in sheer scale for its own sake is linked to the obsession with GNP, which measures the 'scale' of an economy on the basis that bigger is always better. Similarly, economists imply that the state of the nation is linked inextricably to the profits of the largest corporations, or to the level of the stock markets. Little attention is paid to the thousands of small businesses whose profits are not reported by the financial press and whose success is not measured in any index of stocks and shares. Macrophilia fails to allow for the small fry of economic life and thus excludes a substantial proportion of the population from its economic calculations and planning.

Schumacher wrote of 'a crisis in the reactions of human nature to our economic way of life which worships giantism and threatens to submerge the human person'. In other words, size matters, but not in the way that the economists imagine. It matters not because big is best but because small is beautiful. 'After all,' Schumacher continued, 'people are small in size and can confidently cope only with people-sized problems. Giantism in organization as in technology may occasionally give them a feeling of elation, but it makes them unhappy. All modern literature is full of this unhappiness, and so is modern art.'[4]

Smallness within Bigness

At this point, economic 'realists' will argue that such complaints are out of touch with hard realities. Economies of scale do exist, whether we like it or not, and large corporations will always be necessary. Schumacher was well aware of these 'hard realities' and he developed a Theory of Large-Scale Organization to address the issues which they raised. Giant organizations may be inescapably necessary but that did not mean that they could not strive to attain 'smallness within bigness'. To illustrate the point, Schumacher cited the example of General Motors. Its continued success, Schumacher argued, was due to its structuring itself 'in such a manner that it became, in fact, a federation of fairly reasonably sized firms'.[5]

Something similar was attempted in Britain by the National Coal Board, which was one of the biggest firms in western Europe. Under the chairmanship of Lord Robens, 'strenuous efforts were made to evolve a structure which would maintain the unity of one big organization and at the same time create the "climate" or feeling of there being a federation of numerous "quasi-firms". The monolith was transformed into a well-coordinated assembly of lively, semi-autonomous units, each with its own drive and sense of achievement.'[6] Having given these practical examples, Schumacher countered the 'realists' by stating that it was their own theoretical 'idolatry of large size' which was out of touch with reality. For 'practical people in the actual world' there was a tremendous longing for 'the convenience, humanity, and manageability of smallness'.[7]

Giantism in commerce and industry represented a serious danger to the integrity of the individual, who had been reduced to little more than a tiny dehumanized cog in a vast impersonal machine. Yet it also represented a danger to efficiency and productivity, arising out of the growth of Parkinsonian bureaucracies:

> Nobody really likes large-scale organization; nobody likes to take orders from a superior who takes orders from a superior who takes orders ... Even if the rules devised by bureaucracy are outstandingly humane, nobody likes to be ruled by rules, that is to say, by people whose answer to every complaint is: 'I did not make the rules: I am merely applying them.'[8]

Subsidiarity

Since large-scale organizations seem to be here to stay the fundamental task is to achieve smallness within them. Schumacher developed a theory aimed at carrying out this task. Central to the theory was the Principle of Subsidiarity, which stipulated that it was wrong to assign to higher levels in the organization those functions which could be carried out lower down. Schumacher based this aspect of his theory on the 'principle of subsidiary function' promulgated by Pope Pius XI in his encyclical *Quadragesimo Anno*: 'It is an injustice and at the same time a grave evil and disturbance of right order to assign to a greater and higher association what lesser and subordinate organizations can do. For every social activity ought of its very nature to furnish help to the members of the body social and never destroy or absorb them.'

Although the Pope had intended this principle to be applicable to society as a whole, Schumacher applied it specifically to functions within large organizations. In practical terms this meant that large organizations should consist of many semi-autonomous units, which he called quasi-firms. Each of these should be given a great degree of freedom to offer the greatest possible encouragement to creativity and entrepreneurship.

Schumacher symbolized this subsidiarist structure in terms of a man holding a large number of balloons in his hand. Each of the balloons has its own buoyancy and lift so that the man only has to stand beneath them, holding the strings in his hand to keep them together. Each balloon is both an administrative and an entrepreneurial unit, minimizing bureaucracy and maximizing innovation. In contrast, the monolithic structure could be likened to a juggler. Since everything depends on the ability of one man to juggle, he will be more likely to drop the balls when more are added, i.e. the larger the organization the less likely that the all-powerful centre will be able to manage its component parts efficiently.

Since the principle of subsidiary function promulgated by Pius XI was intended to be applicable to the whole of society, it follows that its application should not be restricted to the area of large-scale organizations. In the wider economic context, subsidiarity means that large-scale organizations should be the exception and not the rule. This requires a fundamental shift in the way that economists and politicians view the economy. Economic policy should favour small businesses and should discourage mergers and acquisitions far more robustly than at present. The tax system should be reformed so that the profits of small companies are taxed at a lower rate than those of larger concerns. In short, inverse economies of scale should prevail.

Small Is Bountiful

In spite of the bias of the present system in favour of the big, small businesses continue to thrive. An average of 1,000 new businesses were started every day in Britain during 1999. According to the Government Statistical Office there were 3,708,000 registered businesses in the UK in 1997, of which only 7,000 were classified as large, i.e. with more than 250 employees. Small businesses, including those made up of sole traders or partners without employees, accounted for more than 99 per cent of businesses.[9] Small is not only beautiful, it is bountiful. These extraordinary figures show the true extent to which people want real control over their own lives. They illustrate the yearning for human-sized activity where individuals can be in charge of their own destiny.

One of the heaviest burdens on these multifarious small businesses is over-regulation by the state. 'No one piece of legislation is completely unworkable or unbearable for small firms,' reported a spokesman for the Federation of Small Businesses, 'but it is the cumulative effect of regulation on small businesses which impacts on time, costs money and damages competitiveness.'[10]

The tax system bears particularly heavily on small businesses because they do not have the elaborate schemes for minimizing tax that big businesses enjoy. As such, small companies pay disproportionate levels of tax compared with their larger competitors. In order to address and rectify this anomaly a survey by the Manchester Business School, with help from NatWest and the Federation of Small Businesses, proposed that the government should compensate small companies for administering PAYE and National Insurance and that they should raise the VAT threshold from £51,000 to at least £100,000. Furthermore, the survey proposed that £5,000 or 25 per cent of profits, whichever is the higher, should be tax free if left in the business for all companies with profits of less than £100,000 a year.[11]

And in February 1999 Tony Miller, the Federation of Small Businesses' financial affairs chairman, suggested more fiscal initiatives when he criticized successive governments for failing to help the small business sector. 'The Chancellor reduced the level of corporation tax in the last two Budgets, yet nothing has been done on taxation for the unincorporated business sector, to which the typical small firm belongs. If any Government policy is intended to target small businesses then it must aim for this sector. Successive governments have failed to understand this.' Mr Miller also advocated a 'tax holiday' for new businesses, proposing that any tax chargeable on the first year's profits could on application be deferred and paid by instalments at an interest rate equivalent to the inflation rate over a period of ten years. 'The Treasury will not lose out and it will give new businesses a much-needed lifeline in their early stages when they are often strangled by red tape,' explained Mr Miller.[12]

These are precisely the kind of proactive policies that would encourage the inverse economies of scale required for small businesses to flourish. Yet, with government economic priorities still governed by macrophilia, it is unlikely that such proposals will be acted upon. Instead, with over-regulation still rife, it is hardly surprising that half of new small businesses cease trading within the first three years.

The struggle of small businesses to survive and prosper in the hostile environment created by the macrophilia of central government and the giantism of corporate competition is at the heart of the crisis facing the economy. It is a struggle between human-scale endeavour and inhuman economies of scale. Ultimately, it is a struggle that encapsulates the difficult choice facing humanity as it moves into an uncertain future: the choice between the structural downsizing of the economy and unbridled multinational expansion.

1 G.K. Chesterton, *The Outline of Sanity*, London: Methuen & Co., second edn., 1928, p. 19.
2 Toffler, *The Third Wave*, p. 55.
3 Quoted in Toffler, *The Third Wave*, p. 450.
4 Schumacher, 'Does Economics Help?', p. 36.
5 Schumacher, *Small Is Beautiful*, p. 53.
6 Ibid.
7 Ibid.
8 Ibid., p. 202.
9 *Daily Telegraph*, 20 September 1999.
10 Ibid.
11 *Daily Telegraph*, 11 October 1999.
12 Federation of Small Businesses press release, 8 February 1999.

8

Small Beer: a Case Study

One could see the hops in the tankard, and one could taste the barley, until, more and more sunk into the plenitude of this good house, one could dare to contemplate, as though from a distant standpoint, the corruption and the imminent danger of the time through which we must lead our lives. And, as I so considered the ruin of the great cities and their slime, I felt as though I were in a sort of fortress of virtue and of health ... And I thought to myself: 'Perhaps even before our children are men, these parts which survive from a better order will be acceptable as models, and England will be built again.'[1]

Hilaire Belloc

Probably the most dramatic embodiment of the economic struggle between smallness and giantism in Britain in the years since Schumacher's book was written can be found in the brewing industry. In 1973, the year that *Small Is Beautiful* was published, brewing in Britain was dominated by a few corporate giants. For well over a century the number of breweries had been declining steadily as a few large companies consolidated control. Between 1959 and 1963 this handful of conglomerates had grown rapidly through merger and acquisition. In 1967 there were 244 brewers in Britain. Three years later this had shrunk to 96 brewery companies with 177 breweries in total. By 1973 no new brewing company had been established for fifty years in what was considered a closed industry. The few remaining giants seemed to be completely at liberty to carve up the market between them. In 1976 the largest seven breweries accounted for 91 per cent of all sales of beer. The surviving small breweries looked apprehensively towards a grim future where bankruptcy or acquisition by one of the industry's giants was the likely prospect. Yet, against all odds, there are now well over three hundred new brewers in Britain, over and above the few survivors, producing real ale on a small scale.

The unlikely victory gained by the Jacks of the microbreweries over the giants of the corporate brewing industry is due in large part to the efforts of CAMRA, the Campaign for Real Ale. The idea of a campaign to revitalize British ale arose when four friends from the north-west of England found themselves bemoaning the state of British beer and pubs during a holiday in Ireland in 1971. By this time the corporate giants were seeking to eliminate many traditional ales so that they could concentrate production on a handful of mass-produced, heavily advertised national brands. Not surprisingly, this harmonization of production harmed the product, creating bland, carbonated, tasteless beer which epitomized what G.K. Chesterton called 'standardization by a low standard'.

As their favourite ales disappeared to make way for these substandard substitutes, many drinkers joined the embryonic campaign established by the four friends. By October 1973 CAMRA had five thousand members. Its voice was beginning to be heard. Three years later, with CAMRA membership reaching nearly 30,000, the big brewers were forced to take notice. Ind Coope responded to the growing demand for traditional real ale by launching Burton Ale into a thousand pubs simultaneously. Bass followed by promoting real ale in over a thousand of its pubs in the north-west of England, and Trust House Forte introduced real ale into fifty-two of its outlets. Following such dramatic successes, CAMRA was acclaimed by Michael Young (now Lord Young of Dartington), president of the Consumers' Association, as 'the most successful consumer movement in Europe'.[2]

David and Goliath

This, however, was not the end of the story. CAMRA's success did more than merely force the large producers to respond to consumer demand. It also encouraged the sudden appearance of a host of new micro-breweries which went into competition with the corporate brewers with the bravado and faith of a David facing a Goliath.

At first, in the early 1970s, only a handful of micro-breweries were established. Then, slowly, the numbers began to increase. In 1977 six fresh ventures appeared, with seven emerging in the following year. The new brewers came from all walks of life. Some were devoted real ale drinkers and CAMRA members inspired by a labour of love, others were experienced brewery executives who, disillusioned with the way the large breweries were going, struck out on their own. An example of the latter was Simon Whitmore, who resigned his prestigious post as managing director of Courage Western to establish the Butcombe Brewery in 1978. More than two decades later the Butcombe Brewery continues to produce quality ales at its small brewery in the west of England.

Crucially, a small number of experienced brewers began to act as consultants, providing the equipment and expertise to allow others to become brewers. Peter Austin, former head brewer of Hull Brewery, not only established his own Ringwood Brewery but helped to set up over forty micro-breweries in only ten years. In 1982, Peter Shardlow and Robin Richards took early retirement from Whitbread to form their own brewing consultancy company. In their first year alone, they installed ten breweries. The micro-revolution in the brewing industry had begun in earnest. By the early 1980s the trickle had become a flood. Sixteen new breweries came on stream in 1979, eighteen in 1980, thirty-six in 1981, thirty-two in 1982...

By the end of the 1990s there were over four hundred small brewers throughout the country, brewing high-quality beers for local markets and local tastes, and creating many local jobs in rural or economically marginalized areas. A typical example is that of the Hambleton brewery in North Yorkshire. It was founded by Nick Stafford and his wife Sally in March 1991 at a time when the UK was in the grip of a deep economic recession. Nick had been made redundant twice in the space of seven months and was in desperate need to keep his family and home together. Under pressure he hatched the idea of opening a brewery, which was based initially in converted outbuildings at his wife's parents' home in the tiny hamlet of Holme-on-Swale. Despite the cramped conditions, the brewery achieved its aim of producing 800 gallons a week within the first six months of business.

Before the end of its first year of production, the Hambleton brewery had won a coveted award for the quality of its ale. This initial success continued and within four years Hambleton Ales was employing five members of staff recruited from the villages around Holme. By late 1994 space was becoming a problem and the company moved to a large barn at the other end of the village. Five years later, Hambleton Ales provides employment for ten people in a rural area which has little industry. The brewery now produces 2,500 gallons (20,000 pints) a week and bottles its own brands and those of many other small breweries in the north of England. Its brewing methods follow traditional guidelines, using local malted barley and English-grown hops.

The Empire Strikes Back

It was not long before the big brewing empires struck back against the micro-breweries. Some initiatives were honourable, such as the establishment of home-brew pubs, but others were less so. Most insidious was the offering of cheap loans to strug-gling pub landlords in return for 'brand loyalty'. Small brewers did not have the financial muscle to keep their ales on sale in these pubs when faced with representatives from the big brewers waving cheque books. 'It is all very wrong,' complained Peter Austin of the Ringwood Brewery. 'These sort of loans are illegal in America and Germany, and it's about time something was done about them here.'[3] In this way, through the unethical abuse of their 'economies of scale', the brewing giants deprived the public of the locally produced, quality products they wanted. It was the distortion of local demand to satisfy corporate supply.

A similar abuse was the way in which the big brewers used the tied-house system to exclude the beers of the micro-brewers from thousands of pubs. Ian Hornsey, of the Nethergate Brewery in Suffolk, stated in 1988: 'The tied-house system means that, in our area, eighty per cent of the market is closed to us.'[4] Inevitably, the success rate of the micro-breweries was linked to the extent to which the big brewers were successful in excluding them from the market. In the south-west of England micro-breweries flourished because of the widespread free trade in the region. Yet in areas dominated by the major brewers life could be very difficult. In Wales, out of eighteen bold attempts, only two small brewers still survive.

Parallel with these attempts to strangle the micro-breweries at birth, the Brewers' Society, which represents the vested interests of the major brewers, refused to accept the new brewers as members. In response, the Small Independent Brewers Association (SIBA) was formed in 1980 to help the new brewers fight their corner. Efforts by SIBA and CAMRA to raise awareness of the problems confronting small breweries were rewarded when the government instructed the Monopolies and Mergers Commission to investigate the supply of beer in the UK. Initially the Monopolies Commission proposals included a threat to ban restrictive loans, but this was ultimately dropped. Nonetheless, in May 1990 tenants of pubs tied to the major breweries were given the right to stock a guest ale of their choice. It was a significant breakthrough. The ability of the giants to exclude the micro-breweries from the market had been lessened.

The giants, however, were far from vanquished. They responded by dumping beer into the guest ale market, offering cash discounts that were often in excess of the gross profit margins of their micro-competitors. There was also a threatened legal challenge from the European Commission which was averted in March 1997 through the campaigning efforts of CAMRA. By 1998 membership of CAMRA had reached 52,000, rising to 54,000 in 1999, ensuring that the micro-brewers continued to have a powerful ally in their battle to hold their own in the fiercely competitive market. Meanwhile, the big brewers carried on acquiring and closing smaller breweries. Between 1988 and 1992 Whitbread closed Wethereds of Marlow, Higson's of Liverpool, Fremlins of Faversham and the

Exchange Brewery in Sheffield. Scottish and Newcastle closed Matthew Brown brewers in Blackburn in 1991, and Carlsberg Tetley closed Tetley Walker's Warrington brewery and the Plympton Brewery in Plymouth, both in 1996. Carlsberg Tetley also closed their breweries in Alloa and Wrexham in 1999.

Merger Mania

Apart from this slaying of small breweries by the industry's giants, a few smaller would-be giants, such as Greene King, are joining in the merger mania. In July 1999 Greene King bought Morland's Brewery at Abingdon in Oxfordshire and promptly announced that it would close it. 'Consolidation is killing Britain's independent brewing sector as everyone in the industry seems obsessed with getting bigger,' said Mike Benner of CAMRA when he learned of Greene King's plans for the Oxfordshire brewer.[5]

Clearly the struggle for survival of the micro-brewers and the real ale they produce is not won. The latest marketing ploy of the giant brewers is to ignore real ale in favour of lagers and 'smoothflow, creamy' beers, known as nitro-kegs, which are promoted in multi-million-pound advertising campaigns. The cost of advertising means that its power can only be enjoyed by the largest brewers, so that the public is inundated with enticements to switch from real ale to its mass-produced artificial substitutes.

CAMRA and the Small Independent Brewer's Association have responded to this latest onslaught by calling for the government to adopt a sliding scale of beer duty to protect Britain's small brewers and enable them to compete against the economies of scale enjoyed by the giants. Beer duty in Britain is already far higher than in other parts of Europe and the rate of tax hits the small brewer harder than its larger rivals. Without the introduction of a sliding scale to alleviate the burden, small brewers will find it increasingly difficult to compete in an ever-consolidating market.

The lower rate of beer duty for smaller brewers would offer a progressive solution to the problems they face, creating inverse economies of scale and enabling them to compete on even terms with the giants. The principle is similar to VAT, where companies below a certain threshold are exempt from payment, and to income tax, where the low paid pay a lower rate of tax. Similar systems already exist in many other European countries including Belgium, Germany, the Netherlands, Finland, Austria, Denmark, Portugal and Luxembourg. In Germany the implementation of a sliding scale has helped preserve many of the country's traditional family firms. In practical terms, the cost to the Treasury of such a system would be minimal. The brewing industry raises some £11 billion for the Treasury and the implementation of a sliding scale would cost less than £10 million – less than 0.1 per cent. Consequently, a negligible effect on government revenue could have an enormous effect on the future of small brewers.

A sliding scale would enable small brewers to compete with larger companies on price, leading to a wider selection of cheaper beers. It would enable small brewers to invest in their businesses and play a larger part in developing healthy local economies. It would also improve cash flow, a major problem for small businesses. In short, a sliding scale would promote choice and investment at the local level, creating jobs in otherwise depressed areas.

Besides choice and local colour, the new brewers have also added the vital ingredients of health and quality to beer production. In an era of growing demand for natural, chemical-free products, almost all the new ventures use only traditional ingredients including a high proportion of local malted barley and whole hops. They have no need for the chemical preservatives and head-foaming agents used by the giants in their processed beer factories. They have made brewing a craft again rather than an industry. 'Significantly,' writes Brian Glover, a journalist and former editor of CAMRA's monthly newspaper, *What's Brewing?*, 'when CAMRA campaigned for beer to join other foodstuffs in listing ingredients, the new brewers had no objection and, indeed, led the way in providing drinkers with details of what goes into their pint. In contrast, the major brewers shuffled with embarrassment, evaded the issue, and eventually refused to name their ingredients in a cloud of lame excuses. One is left wondering what they have got to hide.'[6]

Human Scale

The new generation of micro-breweries have also reintroduced an element of human scale in the relationship between brewers and pub licensees. As the giants grow ever larger and more remote from the local pub, small brewers are able to offer a more personal service. 'The man who drives the dray may also be the brewer,' says Glover, 'so the landlord can talk straight to the chap in charge. If a pub runs out of beer at the weekend, only the new brewers have the flexibility – and concern – to deliver. They can even produce a special "house" beer for individual outlets.'[7]

Most surprising, perhaps, is the spread of the micro-brewing revolution to many other parts of the world. After assisting the establishment of small breweries in England and Wales, consultants such as Peter Austin have looked further afield.

Travelling west, Austin helped to establish the Hilden Brewery in Belfast before proceeding to the United States where he helped set up Newman's Brewery in New York state. This in turn sparked a similar micro-revolution in North America. By 1987 the number of new breweries in the United States and Canada had exploded to seventy-five. Similar success followed in Germany, France and Belgium. By the late eighties, Peter Austin was setting up a plant in Nigeria in one month and then travelling to China in the next to set up small communal breweries. Other consultants, such as Peter Shardlow and Robin Richards, helped establish the Palo Alto Brewing Company in San Francisco before moving on to Australia where the Ballarat Brewery became the first new antipodean brewer. Shardlow and Richards also established Italy's first brew-pub in Sorrento and built one in Bavaria for Prince Luitpold von Bayern. They reached beyond the Iron Curtain in 1985, into Hungary, and also established small breweries in Canada, New Zealand and the West Indies.

In the years since Schumacher's book set out the wisdom of small is beautiful, there have been few successes as dramatic as that of the pint-sized response of small businesses in the brewing industry. From the fanciful dreams of four men grumbling into their pints in an Irish pub, the micro-revolution has swept across the world in a way which would have been inconceivable at the time. The subsequent success of their embryonic vision has not only exceeded all expectations but has reached beyond even their wildest dreams.

1 Hilaire Belloc, *Hills and the Sea*, London: Methuen & Co., 1906, p. 290.
2 Roger Protz and Tony Millns, *Called to the Bar*, St Albans: Campaign for Real Ale, 1992, pp. 38–9.

3 Ibid., p. 103.
4 Ibid.
5 *What's Brewing?*, September 1999.
6 Protz and Millns, *Called to the Bar*, p. 106.
7 Ibid., pp. 106–7.

9

Making Democracy Democratic

To the size of states there is a limit as there is to other things, plants, animals, implements; for none of these retain their natural power when they are too large or too small, but they either wholly lose their nature or are spoilt.[1]

Aristotle

'It's hard to equal the language of the ancients,' Schumacher remarked after quoting the above words. Then, echoing Aristotle's ancient wisdom, he reiterated his belief that 'the question of the proper scale of things' was 'the most neglected subject in modern society'.[2] In the two previous chapters we have looked at this subject from the point of view of the economy yet, as Aristotle's words illustrate, its applicability goes beyond economics.

After *Small Is Beautiful* was published, Schumacher received a letter which explained the challenging problem of scale from a mathematical point of view:

The crucial point is that as a monolithic organization increases in size, the problem of communicating between its components

goes up exponentially. It is generally reckoned that the maxi-
mum size of a productive scientific research team is twelve; over
that size everyone spends all his time finding out what everyone
else is doing.[3]

If this crucial point is valid, and Schumacher clearly believed that it was, its implications are manifold. At the beginning of chapter 5 of *Small Is Beautiful*, entitled 'A Question of Size', Schumacher discussed the political implications associated with scale. He had been brought up to believe that the politics of scale were as powerful as the economies of scale. Such was the dogmatic assertion that the politics of scale were inexorable and inevitable, that history was seen as being determined by them. According to this view, human society began with the family; then families joined together to form tribes; then several tribes formed a nation; then a number of nations formed a 'Union' or 'United States'; finally, the consummation of the entire process would be the formation of a single world government. This concept of political determinism could be called the theory of progressive centralization.

Schumacher confessed the apparent plausibility of such a line of reasoning but questioned its ultimate validity. If the process was as inevitable as its proponents claimed, why was there such a proliferation of nation states? Schumacher cited the example of the United Nations Organization. When it had been formed it had some sixty members. Twenty-five years later, when Schumacher was writing, this number had more than doubled and was continuing to grow:

In my youth, this process of proliferation was called
'Balkanization' and was thought to be a very bad thing.
Although everybody said it was bad, it has now been going on

merrily for over fifty years, in most parts of the world. Large units tend to break up into smaller units. This phenomenon, so mockingly the opposite of what I had been taught, whether we approve of it or not, should at least not pass unnoticed.[4]

In the years that have elapsed since Schumacher wrote these words, the phenomenon has continued apace, most notably of course with the break-up of the Soviet empire.

The Politics of Scale

The theory of progressive centralization was itself driven by the theory of the politics of scale. Schumacher had been brought up on the theory that a country had to be big in order to be prosperous – the bigger the better. As with the theory of progressive centralization this appeared to be plausible. Winston Churchill had derided 'the pumpernickel principalities' of Germany prior to the birth of the Bismarckian Reich. It was only through unification under Bismarck that German prosperity was possible. At least that's how the theory goes. Once again, however, Schumacher offered a cautionary counter-stance: 'the German-speaking Swiss and the German-speaking Austrians, who did not join, did just as well economically, and if we make a list of all the most prosperous countries in the world, we find that most of them are very small; whereas a list of all the biggest countries in the world shows most of them to be very poor indeed. Here again, there is food for thought.'[5]

Having offered these practical examples, Schumacher later proffered hypothetical examples to illustrate the same point: 'Imagine that in 1864 Bismarck had annexed the whole of Denmark instead of only a small part of it, and that nothing had happened since ... Or imagine Belgium as part of France.'[6] In the intervening years, the Danes and the Belgians, as ethnic minorities, would struggle to maintain their language and their cultural identity. If eventually they began to demand their independence, the political 'scientists' of the big-is-best brigade would dismiss their demands as unrealistic. The Danish and Belgian 'regions' would be derided as 'non-countries', too small to be economically viable as independent nations. In fact, since history has spared us this scenario, we know that Denmark and Belgium are every bit as viable as their larger neighbours.

Nonetheless, and in spite of voices such as Schumacher's, it is still often believed that big is best in politics, as in economics, and that 'Balkanization' is bad. This view has been strengthened by the bloodshed in the Balkans itself in the past decade. From the security of stable political environments, whether in large or small nations, it is easy to deride as 'primitive' or 'bigoted' the issues that divide less stable areas. 'Why can't everyone live in peace?' is a pertinent question, but it is all too often asked only as an exasperated exclamation at the perceived ignorance of others. It is seldom asked as a genuine plea for understanding, and still less as part of a genuine effort to understand.

Why then is the world so riven with conflict? Ironically, it is due in large part to the theory of the politics of scale. 'Balkanization', so derided by those who believe in big is best, is actually the consequence of the politics of scale which they espouse. The problem is caused by those who most vociferously and patronizingly condemn it. Take, for example, the many conflicts that have erupted in the Balkans recently. They have been due principally to the earlier attempt to fuse Serbs, Croats, Slovenes, Albanians and other nations into an artificially large state called Yugoslavia dominated by the Serbs. Yugoslavia's former dictator, Marshal Tito, could only prevent the mounting ethnic tension from spilling over into violence by keeping order with an iron fist. After his death in 1980 the various nationalities began to flex their democratic muscle, demanding autonomy.

Political Giantism

The same problem was caused, on a much larger canvas, by the politics of scale adopted by the Soviet Union. Lenin and Stalin centralized political power in Moscow, annexing or invading neighbouring nations. Estonia, Latvia, Lithuania, the Ukraine, Armenia, Georgia, Moldova, Tadjikistan and many others were swallowed up by Soviet political giantism. Beyond the Soviet border, Stalin consolidated communist power by forcing most of eastern Europe into the Soviet empire. It was all part of the inexorable march to communist world government, or so Stalin believed. The peoples of the communist empire had other ideas. Preferring the beauty of their own small nations to the power of the Soviet bloc, they began to fight for their independence. One by one the nations of the former Soviet empire seceded, toppling the largest and most powerful political empire on earth. All this has happened since Schumacher's words were written, vindicating his observations.

Of course, theories of the politics of scale and progressive centralization are not the sole preserve of communism. The colonial powers in the West have inflicted profound damage around the world, particularly in Africa. The efforts of the imperial powers to consolidate their empires drove artificial frontiers through the ancestral territories of the African tribes. The great Masai nation was divided between Kenya and Tanzania. Similarly, a line was drawn through Somalia, separating part of the Somali people from their brethren and placing them inside Kenya. The result of imperialist meddling in

Somalia, as in so many other parts of Africa, has been anarchy, war and famine.

In recent years the role of empire-builder in Africa has passed from European nations to the United States, whose colonialist impulse surfaced in Somalia in 1991. At first American intervention was ostensibly humanitarian, concerning itself with delivering food to famine-stricken areas of the country. Soon, however, 'Operation Restore Hope' had been transformed into a military operation, dubbed 'Operation Nation Build'. Its purpose, however, had precious little to do with helping to rebuild the Somali nation, as the words of the US ambassador in Somalia made plain: 'There is no more Somalia. Somalia's gone. You can call the place where the Somali people live "Somalia", but Somalia as a state disappeared in 1991.'[7] It is unclear with what international authority the American ambassador declared the right to announce the destruction of Somalia, but to the Somali people the words of Uncle Sam must have sounded suspiciously like those of Big Brother. Either way, the US-led military invasion failed to bring peace or stability, resulting instead in greater depths of anarchy and bloodshed.

The most telling condemnation of the politics of scale is to be found in those who took it to its logical extreme. In the past century the three political leaders who were most obsessed with centralizing power and with empire-building were Stalin, Mao and Hitler. Josef Stalin and Mao Tse-Tung both believed in a communist world government, the consummation of Marxist theories of economic determinism, and Hitler cherished a dream of a thousand-year Reich where the Germanic race would dominate the world. The result, apart from the abject failure of their centralist beliefs, was the murder of millions of people in the name of ideological 'progress'. Stalin and Mao are believed to have been responsible for the deaths of up to a hundred million people. Although Hitler's tally was considerably less, he would surely have added many more to the total if military defeat had not intervened. The tyrannical trio of Stalin, Mao and Hitler took the politics of scale to its logical conclusion, ditching human-scale politics in favour of the grossest inhumanity imaginable.

Politics As If People Matter

Clearly the legacy of political giantism in the twentieth century leaves much to be desired. What then is the alternative? Essentially it is that the principle of small is beautiful must apply to politics as much as to economics. Whereas believers in the politics of scale call for centralization, politics as if people matter demands decentralization. Whereas believers in big is best look towards the evolution of ever larger, supra-national political bodies to govern humanity, those who seek the human scale in human affairs call for devolution of power to smaller nations or to regions within nations.

Schumacher insisted that the question of 'regionalism' was one of the most important problems facing humanity:

> But regionalism, not in the sense of combining a lot of states into free-trade systems, but in the opposite sense of developing all the regions within each country. This, in fact, is the most important subject on the agenda of all the larger countries today. And a lot of the nationalism of small nations today, and the desire for self-government and so-called independence, is simply a logical and rational response to the need for regional development. In the poor countries in particular there is no hope for the poor unless there is successful regional development, a development effort

outside the capital city covering all the rural areas wherever people happen to be.[8]

In economic terms the regional development to which Schumacher is referring is linked to the application of intermediate, or appropriate, technology (see chapters 14 and 15). In political terms it refers to the establishment, or re-establishment, of genuine small-scale local and regional self-government. It is a call for the re-emergence of genuine democracy.

Since democracy is a political dogma to which most governments in the world claim allegiance, it is necessary to differentiate between nominal democracy and the genuine article. Nominal democracy, the form practised in many of the world's largest countries and in supra-national bodies like the European Union, works more in theory than in practice. At best it is inefficient and inadequate; at worst it is little more than a sham. In order to understand what is meant by genuine democracy it is helpful to reiterate the words of Aristotle which Schumacher quotes with such respect: 'To the size of states there is a limit as there is to other things, plants, animals, implements; for none of these retain their natural power when they are too large or too small, but they either wholly lose their nature or are spoilt.' Not only are Aristotle's words singularly appropriate to the political situation in the modern world, they are sublimely apt since it was, of course, the ancient Greeks who invented democracy. Furthermore, the original Greek model of democracy is still an invaluable means of testing the extent to which modern equivalents live up to the name.

The purpose of democracy for the inhabitants of the ancient Greek city states was to give a voice to every free citizen, not merely in principle but in practice. Every citizen was his own representative and could get up and express his views in the city council. This, of course, was possible because the city states of ancient Greece were relatively small and also, of course, because not every inhabitant was a citizen – some were slaves who had no political rights. Nonetheless, in ideal terms, pure democracy exists when the principle is incarnated into the practice as it was in ancient Greece. Every citizen should be their own representative with both the theoretical right and the practical ability to express their views and influence their community. So far, so good. Most, if not all, advocates of democracy would agree with such a principle.

The Theory of Progressive Centralization

The problems arise when human societies become more complex or, more specifically, when they merge into ever larger political units. When the politics of scale apply there is little option for individuals but to delegate many of their democratic functions to larger institutions. In short, democracy becomes subject to the theory of progressive centralization. Individuals delegate their democratic functions to a local council; the local council delegates its functions to a county council; the county council delegates to the regional council or government; the regional council or government delegates to the national government; the national government delegates to a continental union; and finally, so the theory implies, the continental union will delegate to a world government.

Such a theory leads one a long way from the original Greek model of democracy. Indeed, to what extent will the individual be able to influence a world government? Each of us is but one voice in an electorate of several billion. Clearly our democratic function will only exist as an abstract theory, a human 'right', leaving us with no practical ability to influence the society in which we live. Seen in this light, the theory of progressive centralization is, in relation to democracy, the practice of progressive usurpation. World government usurps the functions of continental unions; continental unions usurp the functions of national governments; national governments usurp the functions of regional authorities; regional authorities usurp the functions of county councils; and county councils usurp the functions of local councils. It is standing the principle of democracy, as conceived by the Greeks, on its head.

This whole issue was discussed with polemical power by John Seymour, doyen of the self-sufficiency movement, in *Bring Me My Bow*. In a chapter entitled 'The Horrible Disease of Gigantism', Seymour let rip rhetorically against those who have usurped power in the name of democracy:

> *What is the cure for this beastly disease of gigantism? Break 'Great Britain' and the other huge nation-states up again. What do we want to be 'Great' for any more? I don't want to be 'Great' – I want to be wise, I want to be free, I want to be kind, I want to be happy. In what did our 'Greatness' consist anyway? In beating other people up and then saying to them: 'Look – we're the bosses of the Greatest Empire the World has ever seen!' Did this make the average Englishman wise, free, kind and happy?* [9]

Seymour's robust denunciation of imperialism was motivated by a profound commitment to genuine democracy in the sense that the Greeks would have understood it: 'The unit which is small enough for every man to make himself personally heard is the only unit that can possibly claim to be a democracy.'[10] Seymour's democratic sensibilities and his belief in the break-up of Great Britain led him to dismiss the two major parties as intrinsically tied to theories of 'gigantism': 'Fortunately, because I live in Wales, my choice is clear. I shall vote for Plaid Cymru, the devolutionist party. My men will not get in, but at least my tiny little voice will be heard, speaking out in favour of a country of humane size.'[11] These words were written in 1977 when devolution seemed little more than a distant dream held by a few eccentric nationalists. Today Plaid Cymru has emerged as a major force in Welsh politics, and devolution, albeit only in a partial and emasculated form, has become a reality.

Yet Seymour, though he lived in Wales at the time, was an Englishman who loved his own country. England, like Wales, was distinct from Great Britain and should be liberated from it. Seymour, however, went still further: 'I have another sort of pride, more private, more intimate, more my own perhaps, and that is in being an East Anglian. Ah, there could be a country! And to be a countryman of East Anglia would in no way lessen my pride at being an Englishman … East Anglia *is* a nation, and as large as any nation ought to be.'[12]

Seymour's characteristic candour will lead many to deduce that he is little more – or less – than a short-sighted romantic, and clearly it is questionable whether the concept of 'nation' could be applied to areas such as East Anglia. Yet his call for power to be devolved from central government to smaller regions is valid. He was also enough of a realist to pre-empt the objections of the believers in *realpolitik* who insist that the politics of scale make small nations, or other forms of small-scale government, impractical in the 'real world':

Now I must brace myself for the counterblast from the people who always say, at this juncture of this particular argument:

> 'What we want is not more nations but fewer! We want to do away with nations altogether in fact. All men should unite in one nation, the nation of the world!'
>
> …Surely it can be seen that one government for the whole world, one all-embracing nation would be about as far from real democracy as you could get? If a man cannot make his voice heard in England how the hell is he going to make it heard in the world? Among – what is the latest guess: four thousand million people – how much is the voice of one honest man going to count?
>
> If there is ever a government of the world you can be sure of this: it will be despotism, not only the biggest but also the most despotic.[13]

If, however, this theoretical world government should ever become a reality, it will almost certainly call itself a democracy. People will have a vote even if they don't have a voice. The problem, therefore, is not whether democracy is the way forward – because almost everyone believes that it is – but undemocratic 'democracy'. The challenge for the future is how to make democracy democratic.

1 Quoted in E.F. Schumacher, *Think About Land*, London: Catholic Housing Aid Society, 1973, p. 6.
2 Ibid.
3 Ibid., p. 7.
4 Schumacher, *Small Is Beautiful*, p. 52.
5 Ibid.
6 Ibid., pp. 58–9.
7 *Washington Post*, 4 September 1994.
8 Schumacher, *Small Is Beautiful*, pp. 60–1.

9 John Seymore, *Bring Me My Bow*, London: Turnstone Books, 1977, pp. 52–3.
10 Ibid., p. 52.
11 Ibid.
12 Ibid., pp. 53–4.
13 Ibid., pp. 54–5.

10

A Democracy of Small Areas

That which is large enough for the rich to covet ... is large enough for the poor to defend.[1]

G.K. Chesterton

Alexander Solzhenitsyn, the Nobel Prize-winning author, was a great admirer of *Small Is Beautiful*. As early as 1973, in his *Letter to Soviet Leaders*, Solzhenitsyn had called for a radical reappraisal of the economy which paralleled Schumacher's vision in many key respects. Specifically, Solzhenitsyn detailed the way in which civilization in both the East and the West was in peril – the peril of 'progress':

How fond our progressive publicists were, both before and after the revolution, of ridiculing those retrogrades ... who called upon us to cherish and have pity on our past, even on the most god-forsaken hamlet with a couple of hovels ... who called upon us to keep horses even after the advent of the motor car, not to abandon small factories for enormous plants and combines, not to discard organic manure in favour of chemical

*fertilizers, not to mass by the million in cities, not to clamber on
top of one another in multi-storey blocks.*

The world had been 'dragged along the whole of the Western
bourgeois-industrial and Marxist path' only to discover

> *what any village greybeard in the Ukraine or Russia had
> understood from time immemorial … that a dozen maggots
> can't go on and on gnawing the same apple forever; that if the
> earth is a finite object, then its expanses and resources are finite
> also, and the endless, infinite progress dinned into our heads
> by the dreamers of the Enlightenment cannot be accomplished
> on it … All the 'endless progress' turned out to be an insane, ill-
> considered, furious dash into a blind alley. A civilization greedy
> for 'perpetual progress' has now choked and is on its last legs.*

Even as Schumacher was issuing similar warnings in the West,
Solzhenitsyn was urging the Soviet government to accept its
responsibility as the guardian of the future. Resources had
been squandered, the soil had been eroded, industrial pollution had created contaminated waste lands, but there was still
time to act positively: 'let us come to our senses in time, let
us change our course!' In particular, Solzhenitsyn called for a
human-scale way of life. Against the huge industrial conurbations Solzhenitsyn contraposed life in the 'old towns – towns
made for people, horses, dogs … towns which were humane,
friendly, cosy places … An economy of *non*-giantism with
small-scale though highly developed technology will not only
allow for but will necessitate the building of *new* towns of the
old type.'

Considering the remarkable similarity in approach, it is not
surprising that Solzhenitsyn has called for the re-establishment

of genuine democracy along similar lines to those advocated by Schumacher and Seymour.

Sustainable Democracy

In *Rebuilding Russia* Solzhenitsyn sought sustainable democracy which 'must be built from the bottom up, gradually, patiently, and in a way designed to last rather than being proclaimed thunderously from above...' The failings of liberal democracy – which perhaps should be called macro-democracy – would, Solzhenitsyn claimed,

> *rarely apply to democracies of small areas – mid-sized towns, small settlements, groups of villages, or areas up to the size of a county. Only in areas of this size can voters have confidence in their choice of candidates since they will be familiar with them both in terms of their effectiveness in practical matters and in terms of their moral qualities. At this level phony reputations do not hold up, nor would a candidate be helped by empty rhetoric or party sponsorship.*
>
> *These are precisely the dimensions within which the new Russian democracy can begin to grow, gain strength, and acquire self-awareness. It also represents a level that is most certain to take root because it will involve the vital concerns of each locality: ensuring unpolluted water and air, overseeing housing, hospitals, nurseries, schools, shops, and the local distribution of goods, while also giving vigorous support for the growth of untrammelled local economic initiatives.*
>
> *Without properly constituted local self-government there can be no stable or prosperous life, and the very concept of civic freedom loses all meaning.*[2]

Solzhenitsyn's 'democracy of small areas' was not plucked from the air but was rooted in Russian history. It 'had been practised in Russia for centuries, with the peasant council existing throughout Russian history, while particular periods saw the *Veche* assemblies and Cossack self-government'.[3] In the nineteenth century local democracy in Russia worked on district and provincial levels 'without being rooted in the villages'. This system was destroyed by the Revolution, which replaced these district and provincial institutions with local soviets answerable to the centralized government of the Communist Party.

Solzhenitsyn alluded to the original Greek model of democracy and, in union with Schumacher, expressed a debt to the ideas of Aristotle. He also pointed to the canton system in Switzerland as a model of good democracy in practice. His admiration for Swiss democracy dated back to the 1970s when he was an exile in Zurich. He told the editor-in-chief of the *Neue Zürcher Zeitung* that he admired Swiss democracy because it was organized in small local units, such as the village and the canton. Unlike the centralized democracies in other western countries, the emphasis in Switzerland was on local self-determination and the active participation of the entire population. In this respect, Solzhenitsyn remarked, it reminded him of the democratic system in medieval Novgorod.

In Switzerland a petition signed by 100,000 of its citizens will compel the government to call a national referendum on any issue concerning changes to the constitution. Similarly, a petition signed by only 50,000 people will ensure a public referendum on any proposals presented to Parliament.

Solzhenitsyn repeated his praise of the Swiss political system in an interview on American television in June 1974. Once again there are similarities between Solzhenitsyn's views and those of Schumacher:

> *Swiss democracy has some amazing qualities. First, it is completely silent and works inaudibly. Secondly, there is its stability ... Thirdly, it's an upturned pyramid. That is, there's more power at the local level ... than in the cantons, and more power in the cantons than with the government ... Naturally, one can only admire such a democracy.*[4]

In contrast to the democracies of small areas there are what could be termed the democracies of large areas. In the United States the progressive erosion of the rights of individual states and the consequent rise in the power of the federal government in Washington has caused widespread concern. It is a classic example of the usurpation of democratic function by the larger institution to the detriment of the democratic functions of the smaller. James Buchanan, the American Nobel Prize-winning economist, suggested at a conference on constitutional issues in Paris in 1989 that the United States had evolved into a single state not much different from other centralized states, and that the Founding Fathers could never have believed that the concept of federalism would degenerate to produce such a centralized leviathan.[5]

The Art of Deception

In similar fashion, Europe in its movement towards federalism looks increasingly, in practice if not always in theory, to be proceeding along the same centralist lines as America. The changing role of the European Union is reflected in the changing of its name over the years. It began as the Common Market, then became the European Economic Community, then simply the European Community, and now it calls itself the European Union. The tendency towards tighter control from the centre is obvious and has been disguised over the years by what looks suspiciously like the artful and deceptive employment of Orwellian newspeak.

When Britons were asked to vote in a referendum on whether the United Kingdom should sign up to the Treaty of Rome they were told that they were simply joining a 'common market'. Questions of sovereignty or political interference in domestic affairs were not an issue because, according to the pro-marketeers, we were voting only to join a free trade agreement that would have economic benefits. It is very likely that the electorate would not have voted to join if they were told that they would be signing away sovereignty and political power to a supra-national body based in Brussels. Since there have been no subsequent referenda, there is no democratic mandate for many of the developments in the quarter of a century since Britain joined.

Towards a Secret Society

When the *Guardian* lodged a case before the European Court of Justice in August 1994 complaining of the secrecy in which European decisions were taken, lawyers for the European Council of Ministers responded by stating to the judges that 'there is no principle of community law which gives citizens the right to EU documents'. The lawyers went on to claim that the heads of national governments also had no right to insist on more openness in EU affairs because their declarations were 'not binding on the community institutions'.[6]

With so much closed government and high-level secrecy it was almost inevitable that the European Commission would eventually be rocked by financial scandal. In March 1999 the entire Commission was forced to resign after widespread fraud and corruption were exposed. Perhaps, with the timely reminder of Lord Acton's words that 'power tends to corrupt and absolute power corrupts absolutely', one might have expected calls for the decentralization of power away from the Commission. Instead, less than six months later, there was a call for a massive extension of EU powers into the sphere of criminal law so that 'EU offences' such as multi-billion-pound fraud could be tackled more efficiently. The extension of EU powers into the field of criminal law will inevitably entail harmonization of national legal procedures, signifying another step towards the European superstate.

Similarly, a European single currency will obviously have effects far beyond the sphere of the economy. It will have to be managed centrally, which will necessitate the principal economic strategy for each member state being determined centrally. Consequently, the ability of national governments to direct economic policy in tune with the wishes of their electorates will be weakened considerably, if not actually eliminated. Although leading members of the Confederation of British Industry, which principally represents big business, called for early entry into the single currency at its annual conference in October 1999, it is significant that the Federation of Small Businesses is much less enthusiastic. The FSB has come out unequivocally against European monetary union, as its manifesto makes clear:

> Under the provisions of the Maastricht Treaty, if the UK joined the Single Currency it would be required to hand over a large proportion of its foreign and gold reserves, control of its money supply and policy to the European institution which would be controlled by unelected bankers.

> *There are fundamental concerns with regard to the capital reserves and future funding of UK pension funds.*
>
> *The FSB is opposed to monetary union and a single currency and believes that such a move would strip the UK of a fundamental aspect of its national sovereignty.*[7]

The fact that the CBI, the representative of big business, is far happier with developments within the European Union than is the Federation of Small Businesses is highly illuminating. It seems that big business is able to establish a *modus vivendi* with big government, whereas small business sees large-scale government as intrusive and uncaring. Macro-economics and macro-politics can work in partnership, steamrollering the needs and aspirations of small businesses in the process. This was evident from the section on 'Small Businesses and Europe' in the FSB's manifesto, which stressed that 'the mounting burden of EU regulation has hit the small firms sector very badly'.

Over-regulation

Several examples were given to highlight the plight of small businesses in the wake of over-regulation by the European Union. In Cornwall it had been a custom for centuries to pack herring in barrels, but this had been banned by a Brussels food hygiene regulation. Also in Cornwall, two vineyards with reputations for producing very good wine were forced to close down because they used a grape variety which had been outlawed by an EU regulation as it was out of favour in Europe. Many butchers' shops had closed because profit margins were inadequate to justify the high costs of compliance with EU regulations. Thousands of small businesses in the poultry industry had closed, with the result that the UK now imported chickens from Europe. Small producers of cheese had been forced out of business not only through EU regulation itself but also because of the shortage of milk as a result of the EU quota system.

Having given these examples, the FSB expressed a degree of scepticism about the benefits of EU membership: 'It is impossible to be precise about the number of jobs lost by over-regulation but the FSB feels the numbers to be substantial. The uncertainty provides a good argument for a detailed cost benefit analysis of EU membership.'

Unfortunately, such an analysis will have to surmount the creative use of statistics. For example, in October 1999 the Britain in Europe campaign, spearheaded by Tony Blair, called for an 'honest, clear debate' on the benefits of EU membership and then proceeded to employ arguments which were anything but honest. It pointed to the lavish grants provided by Brussels to pay for such benefits as 'improved fencing' on farms in Northern Ireland but failed to mention that all this money comes from British taxpayers in the first place. Britain pays £11 billion a year, which is about £1.2 million per hour, into the EU budget, only about half of which ever comes back.

The Britain in Europe campaign also claimed that the EU single market 'led to the scrapping of ten million Customs forms for UK firms, saving an estimated £135 million a year'. What it did not say was that the same firms then had to go through the much more cumbersome exercise of filling in the EU's new Intrastat forms, adding an estimated £1 billion a year to their costs.

Within days of the launch of the Britain in Europe campaign, Romano Prodi, the European Commission president, was outlining plans for an increase in centralized control from

Brussels. His recommendations, drawn from a report by a committee of 'wise men' appointed by Prodi himself, would end the right of veto of individual nations, their last remaining guarantee of any measure of independence. It would mean, for example, that Britain would lose the power of veto in crucial policy areas such as taxation. The committee report insisted that the powers of large member states should be drastically curbed to cope with the 'new Europe'. There could be as many as thirty EU members within a decade, Mr Prodi said, creating a Union which would require a new and unprecedented centralization of power in Brussels. Reform of the existing EU treaty was required so that power could be shifted away from member states and towards Mr Prodi's commission. Furthermore, the number of MEPs sent to Strasbourg by existing member states would be cut, to allow space for the new members in eastern Europe. The implications of such a centralist restructuring were made clear by Graham Mather, a former Conservative MEP and the president of the European Policy Forum. 'Prodi is leading from the front towards a centralized top-down system,' he said.

Clearly the macro-democracy envisaged by Romano Prodi is diametrically opposed to the democracy of small areas. Prodi's enlarged European Union of thirty states will have a population of half a billion, twice as many as the United States. It will be governed in practice, as it is now, by an unelected Commission which, if Prodi's recommendations are accepted, will be given even greater powers. Members of the European Parliament, the 'democratic' institution intended to oversee the Commission, already represent huge constituencies. Under the new proposals these constituencies will be made even larger so that a single MEP will 'represent' more than a million voters. Can such a system be called 'democratic' in any meaningful or practical sense?

'Democratic' Dictatorship

In order to deflect criticism that the European Union is becoming a 'democratic' dictatorship, its supporters often declare that the EU is subsidiarist, i.e. that it will not interfere in legitimate areas of local, regional and national government. Even Romano Prodi has stated that small nations and their identities should be preserved. Yet the extent to which EU regulations are encroaching upon every aspect of life serves as a clear contradiction of such claims.

Any number of examples of EU encroachment could be given, but one will suffice. In August 1999 a West Country meat business was threatened with closure because officials did not like the colour of the overalls worn by its employees. Staff at Baker's of Nailsea in Somerset had worn blue overalls for more than twenty years but officials told the owner, Toby Baker, that their colour did not conform with EU hygiene regulations, which stipulate that working dress must be 'light coloured'. The officials ordered him to change the colour of staff uniforms to silver grey. Furthermore, he was informed that if he did not make the specified changes within three months he would be considered in breach of the criminal law and his business would have its licence withdrawn.

Clearly a system which allows bureaucrats in Brussels to dictate the colour of clothing to be worn by employees in small businesses in Somerset cannot claim to be subsidiarist. Subsidiarity, properly understood and acted upon, means leaving to the individual and the family everything that can be done at individual or family level; leaving to local communities everything that can be done locally; leaving to the region everything that can be done regionally; and only putting into the hands of the nation state those things that cannot be decentralized. Whether any function remains which needs to be handed over to supra-national bureaucracies is a matter for debate, but clearly it does not include the power to decide the colour of the clothes that people can wear.

Far from relinquishing more power to an increasingly remote centre, true subsidiarity and democracy requires that many functions of society be devolved to local and regional authorities. A robust and healthy society consists of families and local communities. These are the real building blocks, the micro-models upon which wider society is built. As such, it is vital that local communities not only survive but prosper. If they are not to be swept up into ever larger conurbations, they must have access to, and control of, local amenities. For example, there should be a proliferation of small and medium-sized community hospitals capable of treating commonplace illnesses. Centralization should only be necessary for highly sophisticated and specialized medical services.

Similarly, with regard to education, there should be a prolif-eration of small and medium-sized schools. These should be at the heart of local communities and largely administered by them. Subsidiarity in the field of education must mean that families enjoy a large measure of control over the running of schools. Government of the education system by nationally controlled 'experts' should be replaced by government by a combination of local authorities, teachers and parents. Where the education of children is concerned parents and teachers are the real experts, not politicians or civil servants.

Not surprisingly, perhaps, politicians and civil servants beg to differ. In March 2001, the Belgian finance minister, Didier Reynders, called for an extension of power to the twelve finance ministers within the EU so that they could centrally 'co-ordinate' education and health spending within the euro-bloc.

'This is an explosive proposition,' wrote Ambrose Evans-Pritchard, the *Daily Telegraph*'s Brussels correspondent. 'He is in effect saying that a fully-fledged European government is needed to back up the single currency.'[8]

These examples have been given to illustrate the genuine democratic choice facing society. On one hand there is the move towards the centrally controlled democracy of large areas. On the other there is the alternative offered by the decentralized democracy of small areas. It is a choice between macro-democracies where power is distant and often serves powerful vested interests, and micro-democracies where human affairs are dealt with on a human scale. In this, as in so much else, it is a struggle between big is best and small is beautiful.

1 G.K. Chesterton, *The Napoleon of Notting Hill*, London: The Bodley Head, 1904, pp. 90–1.
2 Alexander Solzhenitsyn, *Rebuilding Russia*, London: Harvill/HarperCollins, 1991, pp. 71–2.
3 Ibid., p. 73.
4 Quoted in Joseph Pearce, *Solzhenitsyn: A Soul in Exile*, pp. 219–20.
5 James Goldsmith, *The Trap*, London: Macmillan, 1994, pp. 72–3.
6 *Guardian*, 31 August 1994.
7 Federation of Small Businesses, General Election Manifesto 1997, p. 33.
8 *Daily Telegraph*, 31 March 2001.

PART 4

Grounded in the Land

11

The Use and Abuse of Land

Among natural resources, the greatest, unquestionably, is the land. Study how a society uses its land, and you can come to pretty reliable conclusions as to what its future will be.[1]

E.F. Schumacher

'The land carries the topsoil, and the topsoil carries an immense variety of living beings including man.'[2] These words from *Small Is Beautiful* should be in the mind of anyone who is genuinely concerned with the future of life on earth. They hold the key to any realistic discussion of the proper use of land. Our future, and the future of our natural environment, is rooted in the soil.

In the years since Schumacher wrote, ecologists have carried out much research into the complex ecosystems that govern and determine the interdependence of life forms. Their research has vindicated Schumacher's insistence that the land is the greatest material resource available to humanity. When *Small Is Beautiful* was published, however, many still believed that human beings had achieved dominance over nature. They could do what they liked with their environment because science and technology would always ensure that they could overcome any difficulties caused by the onward march of 'progress'.

To illustrate this 'progressive' attitude, Schumacher quoted Eugene Rabinowitch, editor-in-chief of the *Bulletin of Atomic Scientists*. 'The only animals,' wrote Rabinowitch, 'whose disappearance may threaten the biological viability of man on earth are the bacteria normally inhabiting our bodies. For the rest there is no convincing proof that mankind could not survive even as the only animal species on earth!' He continued in similar vein:

> *If economical ways could be developed for synthesizing food from inorganic raw materials – which is likely to happen sooner or later – man may even be able to become independent of plants, on which he now depends as sources of his food…*
>
> *I personally – and, I suspect, a vast majority of mankind – would shudder at the idea (of a habitat without animals and plants). But millions of inhabitants of 'city jungles' of New York, Chicago, London or Tokyo have grown up and spent their whole lives in a practically 'azoic' habitat (leaving out rats, mice, cockroaches and other such obnoxious species) and have survived.*[3]

Such a view is typical of scientism, the creed by which science is idolized as the holder of all the answers. In philosophical terms, scientism leads to giantism, the belief that rational or 'scientific' man is the giant who holds the key to truth. All truth is subject to man; man is not subject to the truth. This philosophical giantism leads to the practical giantism that has laid waste to much of the world's resources and created havoc with its biosphere. 'In our time,' wrote Schumacher, 'the main danger to the soil, and therewith not only to agriculture but to civilization as a whole, stems from the townsman's determination to apply to agriculture the principles of industry.'[4] Schumacher singled out Dr Sicco L. Mansholt as the most 'typical representative of this tendency'.

As vice-president of the European Economic Community, as it was then called, Dr Mansholt launched the Mansholt Plan for European Agriculture in 1968. Mansholt criticized farmers as 'a group that has still not grasped the rapid changes in society'. He believed that the 'progressive' approach for most farmers and farm labourers would be to leave the land altogether and become industrial or office workers in the towns and cities. The advantages were obvious because 'factory workers, men on building sites and those in administrative jobs – have a five-day week and two weeks annual holiday per year. Soon they may have a four-day week and four weeks holiday per year. And the farmer: he is condemned to working a seven-day week because the five-day cow has not yet been invented, and he gets no holiday at all.'[5]

Life in Fast-forward

Mansholt's words were from a lecture entitled 'Our Accelerating Century'. The choice of adjective implies that humanity has finally progressed beyond progress itself. The purpose of life is not to go forward but to go faster. Farmers are notoriously conservative and suspicious of change. They invariably want to put the brakes on whenever they perceive that change is occurring too quickly. The 'progressive' man with his foot on the accelerator has no time for the retrograde with his foot on the brake. It is not merely when seated behind the wheel of a car that the foot cannot be on the accelerator and the brake at the same time.

127

The purpose of the Mansholt Plan was to achieve, as quickly as possible, the amalgamation of small family farms into large 'agribusinesses' which would function as 'modern' food-producing factories. This would require a far greater degree of automation, resulting in the maximum rate of reduction in the agricultural population throughout Europe. Consequently, aid was to be given 'which would enable the older as well as the younger farmers to leave agriculture'.[6] The Mansholt Plan, according to a group of economic 'experts' in *A Future for European Agriculture*, 'represents a bold initiative. It is based on the acceptance of a fundamental principle: agricultural income can only be maintained if the reduction in the agricultural population is accelerated, and if farms rapidly reach an economically viable size.'[7] The experts continued:

It is well known that the demand for food increases relatively slowly with increases in real income. This causes the total incomes earned in agriculture to rise more slowly in comparison with the incomes earned in industry; to maintain the same rate of growth of incomes per head is only possible if there is an adequate rate of decline in the numbers engaged in agriculture.

...The conclusions seem inescapable: under circumstances which are normal in advanced countries, the community would be able to satisfy its own needs with only one-third as many farmers as now.[8]

Accelerated Man

As an accelerated man, Dr Mansholt's message to the retrogressive farmers was simple: Get out of the way or get run over.

'No serious exception can be taken to these statements,' Schumacher wrote, 'if we adopt – as the experts have adopted –

the metaphysical position of the crudest materialism, for which money costs and money incomes are the ultimate criteria and determinants of human action, *and the living world has no significance beyond that of a quarry for exploitation*.'[9]

Many farmers did not, however, share the view of the so-called experts. The European Commission had envisaged an element of opposition, stating that the Mansholt Plan 'may even call forth negative reactions'. Yet even allowing for the jargonized understatement of bureaucratic language, this was a serious underestimate of the furore that ensued. Opposition was stubborn and vociferous, particularly in those countries where small family farms were still widely established. In 1994 the Commission was forced to admit that the Plan had 'proved too radical to be politically acceptable'. It was seen 'as destructive of too many family farms'.[10] In France, in particular, there was a bitter reaction, 'as debate took place against a background of concern about the prospects for the farm community, faced by acute problems of transition from a peasant-type, small-scale farming pattern, depending almost exclusively on family labour and making little use of purchased inputs, to larger-scale, mechanized and capital-intensive units'.[11]

If, however, Mansholt's accelerated approach was a little unsubtle, provoking unforeseen levels of opposition, the Common Agricultural Policy achieved most of his aims in a more insidious way. If farmers could not be bludgeoned into accepting the transformation to mechanized agribusiness methods, their support could be bought by administering subsidies to farmers who were 'economically correct'. In effect, by guaranteeing to buy all their produce at a fixed price, the CAP rewarded farmers for producing as much as possible. A system based purely on quantity was bound to encourage farmers to employ intensive methods of production. The long-term health of the soil, and therefore the environment, was sacrificed for short-term subsidized gain; and, as automation gathered pace to maximize output, the drift from the land continued unabated.

A by-product of this produce-and-be-damned approach to farming was, predictably perhaps, the growing of far more food than was needed. By the 1980s Europe was awash with wine lakes and was buried under mountains of wheat, butter and beef. European taxpayers were paying for the production of more food than they could ever possibly eat. (In 1994 the cost to the British taxpayer of the Common Agricultural Policy was approximately £3 billion a year).

The Mad Hatter's CAP

One of the clearest and most succinct expositions of the CAP was given by a thirteen-year-old girl, Alex Johnston, whose views display a disarming combination of wisdom and innocence. Describing the Common Agricultural Policy 'as much like crazy nonsense as the Mad Hatter's tea party', this astute teenager proceeded to expose the follies of the system with a perception that belied her years:

> If a farmer has a farm with beautiful hedgerows and woods, and masses of wildlife, and he loves the land and everything about it, that farmer would obviously look after it. A 'big-business farmer', on the other hand, who only cares about money, would want to squeeze every penny out of every inch of land that he could get his hands on. So if the Government comes along and says it will pay farmers extra cash if they grow more wheat, for example, the big-business farmer will think nothing of destroying all his woods and hedgerows to make one

big field, which will be easier to plough, plant and harvest, and then drenching the empty landscape with weedkillers and insecticides and fertilizers to get a bumper crop.

The 'care-taking farmer', who loves his land will have a terrible choice of either doing the same thing and feeling like a vandal, or growing things which make less free money from the Government, and maybe going broke in the end and having to sell his farm to the big-business farmer who will wreck everything that the good farmer was so proud of. So that the good farmer might just as well have wrecked it himself and got rich on free money. Anybody can see that isn't fair. It is a poisonous idea, including poisoning a good farmer's feelings of responsibility for his land.[12]

The environmental consequences of the intensive farming encouraged by the CAP have been devastating: grasslands have been ploughed, hedges grubbed up, woodland destroyed and ponds filled in. Vast and ugly prairies have been created across swathes of once-beautiful countryside to produce cereal crops destined for grain mountains that no one will eat. Over two hundred of the most important areas for nature conservation – Sites of Special Scientific Interest – are damaged or destroyed each year. In 1990 a government survey revealed an alarming loss of habitats and wildlife species since 1978 in more than a thousand sites throughout the countryside.

More recently, the CAP was responsible for exacerbating the foot and mouth crisis which was estimated to have cost the British economy in excess of £9 billion. The large-scale routine movement of livestock over great distances, which aided and abetted the plague-like spread of the disease, was made necessary because of EU directives forcing the closure of small local abattoirs in favour of fewer, larger slaughterhouses spread more sparsely around the country. Furthermore, ludicrous loopholes in the EU's sheep subsidy scheme (known as the Sheep Annual Premium, or SAP) has resulted in the illicit movement of sheep as desperate farmers fiddle the system to maximize the level of subsidy they receive.

With characteristic understatement, even the former EU Environment Commissioner Carlo Ripa di Meana admitted that the Common Agricultural Policy is an 'ecological failure', and that the damage it is doing is on a par with the environmental damage done by the polluting industries of eastern Europe.[13]

Coupled with the environmental damage is the genetic damage. A leading expert on the impact of agribusiness on the European environment has stated that 50 per cent of all animal and plant species in central Europe are endangered.[14] According to Brian Gardner, an agricultural consultant and director of EPA Associates SPRL, a Brussels-based company, this represents 'the most damning condemnation of man's role in destroying the biological richness of the planet':

Agriculture is, of course, not wholly to blame for this potential genocide. It cannot, however, escape the accusation of being the major culprit responsible for the loss of many important species of plant and animal; it is also said to be squandering by modern breeding methods the genetic reserves of its own industry by eliminating genotypes of useful farm animals and plants that had been accumulated over the centuries. To take one example: most of the many native regional breeds of cattle that once predominated in the farmyards of western Europe have been displaced by the highly bred – many would say over-bred – Holsteins and Friesians that now form ninety per cent of the EU dairy herd.[15]

Perverse Subsidies

Ecological devastation on this scale would be unacceptable by any criteria, even if it could be shown that it kept down prices to the consumer, yet, perversely, the destruction of Europe's landscape and wildlife is actually costing the consumer money. Dr Norman Myers, an environmental scientist, exposed the 'massive distortions in our economies and our environment' caused by what he termed 'perverse subsidies':

> Under Europe's Common Agricultural Policy we pay £500–£600 per taxpayer per year on policies estimated to cost us an extra £300 in increased food prices. We produce grain or butter mountains, which then have to be stored, or in some cases even destroyed, again at our expense. Then we have to take into account the environmental damage that those subsidies can encourage – croplands are overloaded, hedges are grubbed up by wheat farmers to make bigger fields. Pesticides and fertilizers are used – again, often subsidized – only for them to run off into rivers, or drain into water courses, where more taxes are spent cleaning up pollution.
>
> In Europe, some forty-eight per cent of a farmer's revenues are now from varying kinds of subsidies, and we are still suffering environmental damage from agriculture. By comparison, New Zealand, where subsidies were once as high as sixty per cent, has now reduced it to about four per cent, pasture land is beginning to recover from overgrazing, and agriculture is in better economic shape.[16]

It is implicit from Dr Myers's condemnation of the 'perverse subsidies' inherent in the Common Agricultural Policy that he seeks its radical overhaul, if not its complete abolition. The example of New Zealand clearly suggests that a radical shift of policy could be beneficial to farmers and consumers alike.

A Crumbling Cornerstone

Wyn Grant, in his book on the Common Agricultural Policy, called the CAP 'a cornerstone of the EU' but confessed reluctantly that the cornerstone was crumbling: 'It is not a good use of resources to spend over half of its budget on a policy that does not really help to sustain rural life; allows large-scale fraud; increases food prices for consumers; and is environmentally damaging. It is difficult to have confidence in a set of institutions and political processes that produce such an outcome.'[17]

Regarding the fundamental flaws in the reasoning behind the Mansholt Plan and the Common Agricultural Policy, it is impossible to improve upon Schumacher's original words on the subject:

> In the discussion of the Mansholt Plan, agriculture is generally referred to as one of Europe's 'industries'. The question arises of whether agriculture is, in fact, an industry, or whether it might be something essentially different. Not surprisingly, as this is a metaphysical – or meta-economic – question, it is never raised by economists.
>
> Now, the fundamental 'principle' of agriculture is that it deals with life, that is to say, with living substances. Its products are the results of processes of life and its means of production is the living soil. A cubic centimetre of fertile soil contains milliards of living organisms, the full exploration of which is far beyond the capacities of man. The fundamental 'principle' of modern industry, on the other hand, is that it deals with

man-devised processes which work reliably only when applied to man-devised, non-living materials ... The ideal of industry is to eliminate the living factor, even including the human factor, and to turn the productive process over to machines. As Alfred North Whitehead defined life as 'an offensive directed against the repetitious mechanism of the universe', so we may define modern industry as 'an offensive against the unpredictability, unpunctuality, general waywardness and cussedness of living nature, including man'.

In other words, there can be no doubt that the fundamental 'principles' of agriculture and of industry, far from being compatible with each other, are in opposition.[18]

For Schumacher, the *essential* difference between agriculture and industry is 'a difference as great as that between life and death'.[19] Agriculture is primary, whereas industry is secondary. Human life can survive without industry, albeit at a primitive level, but it cannot survive without agriculture.

Health, Beauty and Permanence

Rather than merely a commodity with a price, land is a priceless asset, the jewel in the earth's crown. Our relationship with it should be one of loving care and devotion, not ruthless exploitation. Whereas the crude materialism of economic experts views agriculture as 'essentially directed towards production', its true transcendent purpose is much deeper. For Schumacher that purpose was orientated towards three goals – health, beauty and permanence. Once these three goals are attained, productivity follows almost as a by-product. The meta-economic view sees agriculture as having a trinity of tasks. It should keep us in touch with living nature, of which we are and remain a highly vulnerable part; it should provide expression for our creativity, enabling us to ennoble our wider habitat; and it should bring forth the foodstuffs and other materials needed for a becoming existence.

If only the third of these is seen as significant, the health, beauty and permanence of both ourselves and our environment will suffer. Schumacher went even further, suggesting that they will not only suffer but that they will be in peril of their very existence: 'I do not believe that a civilization which recognises only the third of these tasks, and which pursues it with such ruthlessness and violence that the other two are not merely neglected but systematically counteracted, has any chance of long-term survival.'[20]

Whatever its long-term effects, the economic pursuit of agribusiness to the detriment of agriculture has had many harmful effects in the short term. The 'success' of agribusiness and its obsession with automation has led to a continuing fall in the number of people working on the land. In the United States, 27 per cent of the population were employed in agriculture at the end of the First World War. By the end of the Second World War this had almost halved to 14 per cent. By 1971 it was only 4.4 per cent, and the downward trend continues. By 1995 those employed in agriculture accounted for less than 3 per cent of the workforce.[21]

Similar decline has been experienced throughout Europe and has been accelerated considerably by the Mansholt Plan and the Common Agricultural Policy. Between 1964 and 1989 the number of farm holdings in the United Kingdom fell from 445,000 to 252,000. Since the early 1980s, over 8,000 people have left farming every year. Today only about 1 per cent of the British workforce is employed in agriculture. Inevitably, many of the displaced farmers and farm workers, uprooted from the land, have been forced into the burgeoning cities, where they contribute to the stresses of modern urban existence.

Meanwhile, increasingly alienated by the social atomization and spiritual vacuity of city life, people yearn for the health, beauty and permanence of the countryside. Economic man hankers after the leafy suburbs, willingly commuting great distances every day to and from his home and work. Rural culture is breaking down, forcing country people into the cities; and urban life is breaking down, forcing city people into the country. It is a vicious circle of restlessness, a whirlpool created by the elusive desire for the spiritual wealth that modern economics doesn't even recognize. 'Nobody,' according to Dr Mansholt, 'can afford the luxury of not acting economically.'[22] Yet, as Schumacher observed, the result is that life becomes intolerable for everybody except the very rich.

It is now more necessary than ever to reconcile human life with the natural world in which it belongs. This cannot be achieved by artificial stimulants such as tourism, sightseeing and other leisure activities. It can only be achieved by changing the structure of agriculture in a direction which is the exact opposite of that proposed by Dr Mansholt and other 'experts'. Schumacher again: 'instead of searching for means to accelerate the drift out of agriculture, we should be searching for policies to reconstruct rural culture, to open the land for the gainful occupation of larger numbers of people, whether it be on a full-time or part-time basis, and to orientate all our actions on the land towards the threefold ideal of health, beauty, and permanence.'[23] Yet, Schumacher remarked, the fundamental failure to address the issue of rural reconstruction 'is yet another example of the disregard of human values – and this means a disregard of man – which inevitably results from the idolatry of economism'.[24]

Drug Overdose

The disregard of human values has been paralleled by a disregard for the ecosystems at the heart of agriculture. Large-scale mechanization has treated the landscape with violence, uprooting hedgerows in order to make fields large enough for combine harvesters. The loss of wildlife caused by such destruction has been immense. Similarly, nature is not fertile enough for the agribusinessmen. She has been increasingly poisoned by chemicals to make her more 'productive'. Fertilizers, insecticides and fungicides saturate the soil in ever-increasing doses, doping our mother earth into pliant submission. Yet if it is true that we do not live by bread alone, it is even more true that we cannot live on drugs alone, and nor can the soil on which we ultimately depend. The 'overdose' approach to agribusiness has done enormous harm to the health of the soil, to the health of the food it produces and, therefore, ultimately and inevitably, to the health of those who eat it.

'All this is being done,' wrote Schumacher, 'because man-as-producer cannot afford "the luxury of not acting economically", and therefore cannot produce the very necessary "luxuries" … which man-as-consumer desires more than anything else. It would cost too much; and the richer we become, the less we can "afford".'[25] This is the perverse paradox at the heart of the 'economic' use of land. The poisonous root of the problem.

The disregard of human nature and the destruction of the environment caused by the Mansholt Plan and the ill-conceived Common Agricultural Policy, has led to nothing short of the decapitation of health, beauty and permanence in the name of wealth, profit and the short-sighted demand for instant and transient gratification. Mansholt's Plan has received its just deserts – in both senses of the word. It has begotten the desert it deserves. The soul of the soil has been sold for cash, and farmer Faustus is left to reap the bitter harvest.

1 Schumacher, *Small Is Beautiful*, p. 84.
2 Ibid.
3 *The Times*, 29 April 1972; quoted in Schumacher, *Small Is Beautiful*, pp. 85–6.
4 Schumacher, *Small Is Beautiful*, p. 90.
5 Dr S.L. Mansholt, *Our Accelerating Century*, London: The Royal Dutch/Shell Lectures on Industry and Society, 1967; quoted in Schumacher, *Small Is Beautiful*, p. 90.
6 Quoted in Schumacher, *Small Is Beautiful*, p. 90.
7 Schumacher, *Small Is Beautiful*, p. 92.
8 Ibid., pp. 92–3.
9 Ibid., p. 93.
10 Wyn Grant, *The Common Agricultural Policy*, London: Macmillan, 1997, p. 71.
11 Ibid.
12 Alex Johnston, with Jonathan Porritt, *Lifelines*, London: Red Fox, 1994, pp. 36–7.
13 Brian Gardner, *European Agriculture*, London: Routledge, 1996, p. 165.
14 Ibid., p. 170.
15 Ibid.
16 *Sunday Telegraph*, 14 June 1998.
17 Grant, *The Common Agricultural Policy*, p. 228.
18 Schumacher, *Small Is Beautiful*, pp. 90–1.
19 Ibid., p. 91.
20 Ibid., p. 93.
21 U.S. Department of Agriculture, National Agricultural Statistics Service.
22 Schumacher, *Small Is Beautiful*, p. 94.
23 Ibid., p. 94.
24 Ibid., pp. 94–5.
25 Ibid., p. 95.

12

Chemical and Biological Warfare

I have no doubt that a callous attitude to the land and to the animals thereon is connected with, and symptomatic of, a great many other attitudes, such as those producing a fanaticism of rapid change and a fascination with novelties – technical, organizational, chemical, biological, and so forth – which insists on their application long before their long-term consequences are even remotely understood. In the simple question of how we treat the land, next to people our most precious resource, our entire way of life is involved, and before our policies with regard to the land will really be changed, there will have to be a great deal of philosophical, not to say religious, change. It is not a question of what we can afford but of what we choose to spend our money on. If we could return to a generous recognition of meta-economic values, our landscape would become healthy and beautiful again and our people would regain the dignity of man ...[1]

E.F. Schumacher

Schumacher's love for the land and its life-sustaining properties caused him to reject agrochemical food production in favour of the organic alternative. In 1970 he became President of the Soil Association, Britain's largest organic farming organization. The Soil Association's mission statement explains that it exists 'to research, develop and promote sustainable relationships between the soil, plants, animals, people and the biosphere, in order to produce healthy food and other products while protecting and enhancing the environment'.

When the Soil Association was formed in 1946 its aims ran counter to prevailing trends in agricultural policy. As discussed in the previous chapter, the policy was to maximize output regardless of the environmental impact. This involved a complex series of financial incentives designed to encourage output, including support of the market price, subsidies towards the cost of chemical fertilizers and capital grants for farm 'improvements'. Farmers were urged to specialize, which resulted in the systematic replacement of the traditional mixed family farms of pre-war years by all-arable or all-livestock agribusinesses. Over the next forty years, the use of nitrogen fertilizer expanded sevenfold and completely new forms of animal husbandry emerged, such as indoor pig and poultry units.

Alan Gear, chief executive of the Henry Doubleday Research Association, which, like the Soil Association, is dedicated to organic horticulture and farming, wrote that some of the chemicals used in agriculture had been developed originally as agents for use in biological warfare: 'During hostilities, the Germans had been working on organophosphate-based chemicals, for use in biological warfare. It was found that these nerve gases could, with little modification, be pressed into service as insecticides. Similarly, DDT, which had been used extensively by front line troops, for controlling lice infesting their uniforms, found a ready and expanding market as a novel pesticide.'[2] Thus the chemical research employed in time of war was put to use against mother earth as science declared its own war on nature. New insecticidal organochlorine compounds, such as Dieldrin, Aldrin and BHC, were soon developed, as were new chemical substances designed to kill 'weeds'.

Environmental Hangover

In terms of output, this chemical input proved a great success. Yield increases for cereals, for example, more than doubled. This was due in part to the financial incentives provided by government, which subsidized the increasing dosage of artificial fertilizers, insecticides, fungicides and weedkillers. Parallel with this was the part played by plant breeders in developing a succession of hybrid wheat varieties that responded positively to increased chemical inputs. Unfortunately, however, this 'success' disguised the hidden costs of chemical use. After half a century, the chemical side-effects have caused a considerable environmental hangover:

A recent study for the German government by Hermann Waibel and Gerd Fleischer of the Pesticides Policy Project at the University of Hanover attempted to ascertain the social costs of pesticide use in Germany. The approximate cost to German society of the contamination of drinking water, the loss of biodiversity, the monitoring of food residues, the damage to human health, and the bureaucratic policing of government pesticide monitoring was estimated at between 250 and 300 million DM per year. The report also pointed to additional side-effects of pesticide use which had been identified but not quantified in monetary terms. These included losses through pesticide exposure in other productive areas such as fish farming or poultry rearing; the cost of withdrawing contaminated

goods from the market; the cost of testing imported food for pes-
ticide residues; the cost of chronic illnesses such as cancer; the
effects on 'non-target' animals and plants; and the long-term loss
of sustainability in agricultural production and soil fertility.[3]

The cost of overdosing the land with chemicals in arable farm-ing has been paralleled by the cost of overdosing animals in intensive livestock units. Intensive livestock production relies heavily on the use of antibiotics. The unnaturally crowded and cruel conditions in which pigs and poultry are kept, sometimes spending their entire lives with no natural light and no room to move freely, provide an ideal breeding ground for diseases, which can spread rapidly. These potential disease outbreaks are kept in check by the daily use of antibiotics in a preventive, or prophylactic, way. More than one-third of all antibiotics used are fed routinely to farm animals to prevent the spread of diseases caused by unnatural and cruel farming methods. Even worse, antibiotics are also fed to animals to make them grow faster than nature intended.

Drug Abuse

The consequences of this drug abuse on animals may also prove catastrophic for humans. The effectiveness of antibiotics, the discovery of which was arguably the greatest advance in medical science during the twentieth century, is under serious threat. This is because the more often antibiotics are used, the less effective they become. Their overuse enables the bacterial diseases they target to become resistant to them. Strains of tuber-culosis, meningitis and enterococci have already become fully resistant to all antibiotics, and most food poisoning organisms such as salmonella are highly drug resistant. One in six salmonella infections are now caused by strains resistant to at least four antibiotics. One strain, Salmonella typhimurium DT104, is known to be resistant to seven antibiotics. It infects three thousand people a year and is widespread in cattle and humans. There is serious concern about other so-called 'superbugs', such as VRE, which are resistant to all antibiotics. Medical experts now fear that extremely dangerous bacteria, such as MRSA which affects twenty thousand people a year, could also become resistant.

It has become clear that the abuse of antibiotics in intensive livestock farming is a major cause of drug-resistant disease in humans. The routine dosing of animals with antibiotics allows resistant bacteria to develop inside them, often doubling in number every twenty minutes. Research in Denmark and Germany has shown that resistant bacteria were present in three-quarters of intensive farms, while none were found in organic farms. The effectiveness of antibiotics is being sacrificed to perpetuate intensive systems of agricultural cruelty. Without these drugs, animals could not be kept in such unhealthy conditions and farmers would be forced to adopt more traditional and natural methods of farming, providing their livestock with more space and fresh air.

As a result of campaigning by environmental pressure groups some, but not all, of these growth-promoting drugs have been banned. In 1995 the Soil Association launched a campaign against the growth-promoting antibiotic Avoparcin. Two years later, as a result of sustained pressure, it was banned. By 1998 four of the commonly used growth-promoting antibiotics had been banned throughout the European Union. Yet this has induced many agribusinessmen, stubbornly intent on intensive farming techniques, to seek out other antibiotics to maintain a form of agriculture which is ultimately unsustainable. The Soil Association complained that 'banning only *some* growth-promoting antibiotics is an inadequate half-measure – other similar drugs will be left open to abuse as before'.[4]

The whole problem was encapsulated by Lord Soulsby, chairman of the House of Lords inquiry into antibiotics and farming, on 23 April 1998:

> *Our inquiry has been an alarming experience. Misuse and overuse of antibiotics are now threatening to undo all their early promise and success in curing disease. But the greatest threat is complacency, from Ministers, the medical professions, the veterinary service, the farming community and the public at large. Our report is a blueprint for action. It must start now if we are not to return to the bad old days of incurable diseases before antibiotics were available.*[5]

The Soil Association has continued its campaign to end the abuse of antibiotics in farming, stressing the dangers to human health that it causes. As well as demanding the banning of all growth-promoting antibiotics, it seeks the banning of the routine prophylactic use of antibiotics and the stopping of imports of meat from countries that fail to take similar measures. Yet as Patrick Holden, Director of the Soil Association, stated, 'we need to overcome the combined influence of the drug companies and the intensive livestock industry'.[6]

A similar unholy alliance is behind recent attempts to force genetically modified organisms (GMOs) on to an unwilling and sceptical public. 'The five Major Agrochemical Companies envisage a future where only a handful of varieties of wheat, maize, rice and other food crops are grown commercially,' writes Patrick Holden. 'They are working flat out now to ensure that within a decade most of the world's staple crops will be from genetically modified seeds which they have engineered. As a result, few traditional varieties will be available to farmers. These new strains will only be available from them, at their price. They will be resistant to the most powerful herbicides which farmers will use to kill every other plant in a field, producing a chemical desert devoid of wildlife.'[7] Patrick Holden's words were echoed in February 1999 by Simon Lyster, director general of the Wildlife Trusts: 'Genetically engineered crops made resistant to weedkillers will be sprayed so that all other plants are killed. No plants, no insects, no birds. Genetically engineered crops could turn our agricultural land into a biological desert.'[8]

'Gene Dictators'

Opposition to this latest attack on mother earth has been vociferous. The Soil Association refers to the large agrochemical companies as the 'Gene Dictators' and the tabloid press has dubbed their genetically modified products as 'Frankenstein foods'. It is not difficult to see why the genetic engineers have provoked such an outspoken and forthright response. Motivated solely by the desire to maximize profits, agrochemical multinationals such as Monsanto see GMOs as the key to dictating the future of the global food industry. By using the gene technology which they have patented and can control, they will be able to wield enormous power globally, regardless of the risk of irreversible consequences for human health or the environment.

Combining genetic materials from plants and animals which would never breed naturally could have many serious results. It could jeopardize the safety and quality of food because not enough is known about the way that genes will act, or react, when moved from one species to another. It could endanger wildlife. For example, English Nature has warned that commercial use of genetically modified crops 'could increase … considerably' the widespread loss of farmland birds, the populations of which have been devastated already by chemical farming methods.

Graham Wynne, chief executive of the Royal Society for the Protection of Birds, echoed the concerns of English Nature: 'Any reasonable assessment of the environmental safety of these crops will require a minimum of three years, but the government seems determined to permit the release of the crops after only one year. The fact that Monsanto has now resorted to blaming cats for the decline in farmland birds simply adds to the impression that it is only the environmental groups who are putting forward arguments based on science.'[9] Another RSPB spokesman urged a 'cautious approach', warning farmers that they 'would be very unwise' to rush into the cultivation of GM crops: 'They do not want another BSE or E. coli horror.'[10]

If these words sound a little alarmist, it is interesting to note the worries of many in the medical profession. A poll in the Newsletter of the International Society of Chemotherapy indicated that a clear majority considered the presence of an antibiotic-resistant gene in genetically modified maize an unacceptable risk. Fifty-seven per cent of 198 experts from twenty-five countries believed the risk was unacceptable, while a further 34 per cent believed that more risk assessment was required before the maize was cleared for full-scale use. Only 2 per cent believed the maize to be safe. Yet this type of maize has already been approved for consumption in the European Union and is available in shops throughout the UK. Just two countries in the European Union, Austria and Luxembourg, have refused to import GM maize in defiance of the EU ruling.[11]

Unknown Risks

GM crops could pose a considerable threat to the wider environment because it is impossible to predict the effect that genetically modified plants will have on the wider ecosystem once they are 'released' into the open. 'I have a worry,' wrote Professor Steve Jones, head of genetics at University College, London, 'and it's a biologist's worry because what we've done in this field is to put genes in places they've never been before. And there's a real chance they will get out. And what's going to happen to these genes in twenty years? The answer is we simply don't know. And as we don't know, there is a risk.'[12] Dr Mae-Wan Ho, a biophysicist and geneticist at the Open University, shared the concerns of Professor Jones. She told the BBC's *Today* programme: 'If you look at the scientific evidence, there are already signs that some of the products marketed may be harmful for human beings as well as for beneficial species.' She added that the level of monitoring of GM crops was 'derisory'.[13]

Dr Phil Gates of Durham University, writing in the May 2000 issue of *Gardeners' World*, echoed the fears of many that the emergence of GMOs represented both a potential danger to the environment and a fundamental affront to the rights of the individual:

Any GM crop carrying alien genes from another species needs thorough safety testing before it enters the human food chain. Several years ago, attempts to improve the nutritional quality of soya beans by adding genes from Brazil nuts were abandoned, since these beans then had the potential to trigger reactions in people who had nut allergies.

Public concern now centres on the environmental impact of GM herbicide-resistant crops ... If these turn out to be as efficient as the agrochemical industry claims, then we might see a decline in native wild plants on farmland. This would break the link in a food chain that supports harmless insects and birds, leading to a sterile countryside...

One good argument against GM crops has more to do with civil liberties. Our homes and gardens are our castles, so if we choose to reject GM crops then we shouldn't have them forced on us by scientists and politicians.

But gardeners might not have that choice. Pollen, carried by wind or insects, can travel long distances. Organic growers' livelihoods are threatened by GM pollen contaminating their crops. If you grow sweetcorn downwind of a field of GM maize, then you might unknowingly eat a GM corncob, cross-pollinated by the alien pollen. Drifting pollen may well spread genes from GM crops far and wide.

'Nasty Surprises'

Dr Gates explained that the problem was exacerbated by the fact that oilseed rape can cross-pollinate close relatives that are weeds. If these cross-pollinated weeds should acquire any of the modified genes that are resistant to herbicides the result would be new herbicide-resistant agricultural weeds. There was also a danger that GM pest-resistant crops could cross-pollinate with wild plants, spreading the genetically engineered pesticide genes which could then kill beneficial insects. Dr Gates described such possibilities as 'a serious cause for concern', as were the 'nasty surprises' that have sprung from the testing of GM crops in the United States.

One set of experiments suggested that leaves coated with pollen from GM maize might kill caterpillars of harmless monarch butterflies. More recent tests have shown that GM maize secretes genetically-engineered pesticide toxins through their roots into the soil. These toxins could then kill the beneficial organisms that live around plant roots. It was 'most surprising', Dr Gates added, that 'no one apparently thought to test for this possiblility' before millions of acres of GM maize were planted in the United States. 'Revelations like this do little to boost public confidence.'

A further possible hazard highlighted by Dr Gates is the use of antibiotic-resistant genes in the production of new GMOs. 'Fears over the spread of this antibiotic resistance to bacteria, rendering antibiotics useless for treating humans, have led to an urgent search for safer methods.'

'With so many unanswered scientific questions, perhaps it isn't surprising there is such opposition to genetically modified crops. But the issues run deeper than scientific risk analysis. They concern our right to choose what we grow and eat…'

The ability of people to make informed choices about the food they eat is made even more difficult because some companies have refused to segregate crops which contain modified genes from those which don't. This makes it impossible to have a proper labelling scheme that would enable people to make up their own minds about whether or not they wish to eat GM food. Prince Charles, declaring that 'this kind of genetic modification takes mankind into realms that belong to God, and to God alone', voiced the concerns of many about the need to protect consumer choice from unwanted and unlabelled GM encroachments into the market place:

Obviously, we all have to make up our own minds about these important issues. I personally have no wish to eat anything produced by genetic modification, nor do I knowingly offer this sort of produce to my family or guests. There is increasing evidence that a great many people feel the same way. But if this is becoming a widely-held view, we cannot put our principles into practice unless there is effective segregation of genetically modified products, backed by a comprehensive labelling scheme based on progress through the food chain.

Arguments that this is either impossible or irrelevant are simply not credible. When consumers can make an informed choice about whether or not they eat products containing genetically modified ingredients they will be able to send a direct and unmistakable message about their preferences. I hope that manufacturers, retailers and regulators will be ready to take on the responsibility to ensure that this can happen.[14]

Force-Feeding

Regardless of the degree to which retailers have responded to public demands for information on GM food, the response of manufacturers and regulators has been nothing short of scandalous. The agrochemical multinationals have a clear agenda which does not include the wishes of the consumer. They have invested vast sums of money in the development of a range of new genetic modifications. They are now determined to reap the financial rewards by forcing the world's population to eat genetically modified food – whether we like it or not. In 1994 Monsanto admitted that genetically modified soya and maize, imported from the United States, are to be found in 60 per cent of processed food sold in the United Kingdom, whereas Greenpeace believes a conservative estimate of the true figure is in excess of 80 per cent.[15] It is effectively being force-fed to an unwilling public given inadequate information about the type of food they are being given to eat. Not for the first time, the health of the people and the planet is being put at risk to secure a 'healthy' profit for a few.

The response of regulators to the conflicting demands of multinational muscle and consumer choice has been to side with the giants. GM food was initially introduced without proper public consultation, without segregation of crops and without any labelling. Even after new labelling rules were grudgingly introduced in response to growing public demand it is still difficult to tell whether food contains GM ingredients. Companies are still permitted to call a food GM-free even when it contains two per cent of GM ingredients. In Australia and New Zealand so-called 'GM-free' food may contain as much as five per cent of GM ingredients. No adequate safety testing has been introduced to detect the unpredictable effects of gene modifications. No allergy testing of GM foods is required even though genetic changes may increase the risk of allergens.

Furthermore, the scientific evaluation of GM products is based on evidence supplied by the agrochemical companies wishing to have their products approved. Some GM ingredients, such as enzymes, require no approval whatsoever. No adequate precautions have been drawn up to protect organic farms or GM-free conventional farms from cross-contamination by neighbouring GM crops. Finally, too many government committee members who decide on the future of GM foods and crops have links to agrochemical or food companies.

A Cosy Business Relationship

The cosy business relationship between manufacturers and regulators was epitomized in the composition and procedure of a House of Lords subcommittee which subsequently issued a report strongly endorsing GM foods. Nine of the twelve peers on the committee had an interest in large-scale agribusinesses and one, Lord Joplin, was a shareholder in Zeneca, one of the largest biotech companies involved in genetic modification. Consumer and environmental groups complained that the report was muddled, inaccurate and, above all, biased. The committee had sought evidence overwhelmingly from people who had financial interests in the development of GM technology, such as leading agrochemical and biotech companies, GM lobby groups and institutes with GM-related research contracts. Evidence was also given by the US Department of Agriculture, which is unquestioningly and vehemently pro-GM, by the US Soya Bean Association, representing one of the biggest groups of GM-crop growers, by multinational companies like Unilever and Nestlé, and by academics who, in the words of the *Guardian*, 'fiercely push the technology or sit on government advisory boards known to favour the technology'. According to the *Guardian*, among more than fifty witnesses the peers called on to give evidence, 'there were only two consumer groups, three environment groups and one company known to be doubtful about the technology'.[16] Not surprisingly the Consumers' Association treated the report's findings with considerable scepticism: 'We are concerned about whether this was a genuinely independent inquiry into the use of genetic technology in agriculture. The industry and its friends are entitled to give evidence, but ... the list [of those giving evidence] reflects overwhelmingly the interests of the food industry and of their associates.'[17]

There was a creeping feeling that the debate was being rigged and that the forces of big business and big government were being mobilized to crush any opposition. The opposition, however, was not to be crushed so easily. Against all odds an unexpected alliance of consumers, retailers and small organic farmers would represent a real and growing challenge to the multinational monolith. According to Alan Gear, 'the prospects for farming appear polarized between those advocating sustainable agriculture in harmony with nature, and those others who predict an increasingly hi-tech future of intensive agriculture driven by genetic engineering'.[18] The battle lines are drawn but the final outcome of the struggle remains in doubt. It will be fought between the forces of scientism, who seek to defeat nature through the use of biological and chemical warfare, and those who seek in nature a powerful ally in the sustenance of life. Ultimately it is a choice between the death and the resurrection of the soil.

1 Schumacher, *Small Is Beautiful*, p. 96.
2 Alan Gear, 'Organic and Non-Organic Agriculture', in Janet M. Dalzell (ed.), *Food Industry and the Environment in the European Union*, Gaithersburg, Maryland: Aspen Publishers Inc., 2000.
3 *Pesticides News*, no. 39, March 1998.
4 'Here's why the misuse of antibiotics in farming has got to stop *now* ...', Soil Association leaflet.
5 Extract from House of Lords inquiry into antibiotics and farming, 23 April 1998.
6 'Here's why the misuse of antibiotics in farming has got to stop *now* ...', Soil Association leaflet.
7 'Look what the Gene Dictators are growing just for you', Soil Association leaflet.
8 'Greenpeace True Food Campaign' leaflet.
9 *Genetic Network News*, Issue 4, bi-monthly news sheet of the Norfolk Genetic Information Network.

10 Ibid.

11 Ibid.

12 Quoted in Greenpeace 'True Food Campaign' leaflet.

13 *Genetic Network News*, Issue 4.

14 HRH the Prince of Wales, 'Seeds of Disaster', *Daily Telegraph*,
    8 June 1998.

15 Monsanto gave the figure of 60 per cent in evidence to the Department
    of Agriculture during deliberations preceding the establishment of GM
    field trials in the United Kingdom. The Greenpeace estimate, based on
    independent calculations, is cited in the organization's 'True Food
    Campaign' literature.

16 *Genetic Network News*, Issue 4.

17 Ibid.

18 Gear, 'Organic and Non-Organic Agriculture'.

13

The Resurrection of the Soil

...any society can afford to look after its land and keep it healthy and beautiful in perpetuity. There are no technical difficulties and there is no lack of relevant knowledge. There is no need to consult economic experts when the question is one of priorities. We know too much about ecology today to have any excuse for the many abuses that are currently going on in the management of the land, in the management of animals, in food storage, food processing, and in heedless urbanization. If we permit them, this is not due to poverty, as if we could not afford to stop them; it is due to the fact that, as a society, we have no firm basis of belief in meta-economic values, and when there is no such belief the economic calculus takes over. This is quite inevitable. How could it be otherwise? Nature, it has been said, abhors a vacuum, and when the available 'spiritual space' is not filled by some higher motivation, then it will necessarily be filled by something lower – by the small, mean, calculating attitude to life which is rationalized in the economic calculus.[1]

E.F. Schumacher

The growing perception that government regulatory bodies are in league with the pro-GM food lobby was reinforced by a leaked survey produced by the agrochemical giant Monsanto. The leaked report stated that Monsanto had made significant progress with Britain's political elite, such as Members of Parliament and senior civil servants, but added that public confidence in UK regulatory agencies was in serious decline. The Monsanto survey disclosed that public opposition to genetic modification was 'skyrocketing' in the United Kingdom: 'The latest survey shows an on-going collapse of public support for biotechnology and GM foods. At each point in this project, we keep thinking that we have reached the low point and that public thinking will stabilize, but we apparently have not reached that point. The latest survey shows a steady decline over the year, which may have accelerated in the most recent period.' The report went on to state that 'feeling toward foods with GM ingredients has grown dramatically more negative, which is probably the best measure of our declining fortunes in Britain'.

The Monsanto report claimed that public hostility was being fuelled by the media. It bemoaned the fact that even the 'media elites are strongly hostile to biotechnology and Monsanto. They think the government is being too lax and believe they must expose the dangers.' In Germany the situation was even worse, the report disclosed.[2] Reactions against Monsanto have become so widespread that even the financial markets are responding to the public opposition to GM food production. The stock rating of Monsanto fell to such an extent by early 2000 that Deutsche Bank advised it to pull out of biotechnology.

The combined potency of a hostile media and negative public opinion forced the retailers to act upon GM foods where the regulatory bodies had singularly failed. Retailers were prompted to take action after an extensive survey of customers from all the leading UK supermarkets revealed that 58 per cent were opposed to the stocking of food containing GM ingredients. Sixty-five per cent of Marks and Spencer customers, 63 per cent of Somerfield customers, 61 per cent of Safeway customers and 60 per cent of customers of Sainsbury and Tesco were opposed to the stocking of GM foods by the supermarkets. The majority of customers of Asda, the Co-op, Morrison's and Kwiksave were also opposed to GM foods.[3] More worrying yet for the leading supermarkets was a survey which revealed that 90 per cent of shoppers would change stores if it enabled them to buy GM-free food.

Faced with such levels of public demand, the leading supermarket chains had little option but to respond quickly and decisively. Marks and Spencer, who had previously dismissed concerns about GM food by insisting that its customers were not worried by gene technology, was forced to make a quick and dramatic U-turn, stating that it was 'removing all GM ingredients including derivatives from St Michael food products as quickly as possible'. Sainsbury stated that it was 'committed to eliminating GM ingredients from its own brand products' and Waitrose declared that it would be doing the same.

Susan Bayliss, of Asda customer relations, stressed that the company has 'an approach to genetically modified foods in line with the concerns expressed by customers'. In practice, this meant that Asda had told its suppliers to refrain from using GM soya or maize in new own-label products and to use certified non-GM sources of soya and maize in existing products. If necessary, suppliers were asked to reformulate products to ensure the replacement of GM ingredients with non-GM equivalents. Asda also told its suppliers that it would not accept food products containing any new GM ingredients.[4]

In similar vein, Shirley Kidd, customer service manager for Tesco, acknowledged 'that many of our customers are concerned about foods that contain genetically modified ingredients':

> So far, the feedback we have received from our customers has indicated that they want to be able to make a straightforward choice, based on good information and honest labelling. Therefore, we have decided that, where practical, we will remove genetically modified ingredients from our products, reducing considerably the number of products which contain genetically modified ingredients. We have also pledged to provide increased GM-free options by adding to our organic range.[5]

Moral High Ground

The supermarket chains are continuing to vie with each other for the moral high ground. Iceland pointed out that as early as May 1998 it had become 'the first food retailer in the world to remove GM ingredients from our own-brand products ... long before the media, the government and most of our competitors even recognized there was a problem'. Continuing to blaze a trail, Iceland described themselves as 'retail revolutionaries, willing to fight for what we believe in ... That's why we're continuing our fight for food you can trust by becoming the first food retailer to remove all artificial colours, flavours and, where it's safe, preservatives from all of our own products.'

Iceland's bold initiative won the endorsement of the Hyperactive Children's Support Group, who welcomed the initiative as 'a positive move in the right direction for all those children and adults sensitive to food additives'. It also won the support of Greenpeace, who praised Iceland's eco-friendly approach to retailing: 'Iceland led the way by banning GM foods. Then they led the way by being the first supermarket to sell fridges and freezers which use climate and ozone friendly "Green freeze" technology – which we endorsed. Now they are introducing organic food at little or no extra cost – something else that we've been campaigning for.'[6]

Stung by such a consumer-driven retail backlash, even agribusinessmen have started to pull out of GM food production. In Norfolk, a survey of farmers carried out by the Norfolk Genetic Information Network revealed that almost all farmers who had been growing GM crops on their land had ceased doing so. The UK's largest farming organization, the Co-operative Wholesale Society, had pulled out of all GM crop production and the UK plant breeders CPB Twyford were no longer producing GMOs, a decision attributed to direct action by protesters on their test crops. According to a report on Radio Four's *Today* programme, the number of GM test sites across the country had fallen dramatically.[7]

Despite all the evidence of continued public hostility towards GM foods, Tony Blair's government continues stubbornly to support the production of commercially grown GM crops. Furthermore, in the USA, where the majority of commercial GM crops are grown, there was little public awareness of the issues surrounding GM foods until the issue gained widespread publicity following demonstrations at the meeting of the World Trade Organization in Seattle at the end of 1999. Consequently, with little opposition to the expansion of the GM food industry in the United States, and with the British government still hoping that the industry will eventually succeed in spreading to Europe, the danger of genetic manipulation is as real as ever.

There was, however, a significant victory for the anti-GM lobby at the end of January 2000. An international summit in

Montreal, sponsored by the United Nations, banned GM crops suspected of posing a risk to public health from being imported into 168 countries, including Britain. The summit overcame opposition from the United States to adopt a protocol giving governments the right to exclude GM crops if there is 'reasonable doubt' that they could endanger public health or the environment. A spokesman for Greenpeace described the Biosafety Protocol as 'an historic step towards protecting consumers and the environment from the dangers of genetic engineering'. Pete Riley of Friends of the Earth was delighted that 'the world's governments are finally starting to take control in this very sensitive area by introducing the precautionary principle we have been campaigning for'. He added that until the summit, 'the agenda had been dictated by giant companies, mostly American, but now the American view has been marginalized by the weight of public opinion'.

The Safe Alternative

Public response to the danger posed by GM crops was certainly dramatic in Britain, where it was fuelled and intensified by memories of the calamitous BSE epidemic that had decimated British beef production. Fearful of the possible consequences of genetic meddling and suspicious of government connivance with the GM food lobby, consumers are increasingly demanding organic food as the only safe alternative. Once again, the large supermarket chains have been quick to respond to the demand.

In September 1998 the Soil Association, in partnership with the *Mail on Sunday*, instituted the first Organic Supermarket of the Year award. By the following year, demand had burgeoned to such a degree that Tesco – which sells more organic produce than anyone – announced that organic food was now part of everyone's shopping basket and that the next generation would know nothing else. Even allowing for marketing hype, Tesco's claims seemed to signify a major change in attitude towards organic food on the part of consumers and retailers alike. Sales of organic produce have soared, with some forecasts predicting that as much as five to eight per cent of all food sales will soon be organic. Sainsbury's, Tesco and Waitrose have all doubled or tripled the number of organic lines they stock, and Asda and Safeway are hard on their heels. Smaller supermarket chains such as Somerfield, the Co-op, Iceland and Booths have followed suit. Marks and Spencer, who spectacularly pulled out of organics in the early nineties, was forced into another consumer-driven U-turn, rapidly expanding its selection of organic produce and predicting that organic sales would treble.

Behind the scenes, large retailers began to explore ways of guaranteeing regular adequate supplies of organic produce. The fresh produce buyer for Waitrose informed all his regular potato growers that they should phase out conventional, i.e. chemical-grown, potatoes as soon as possible and switch to organic production. At first these agribusinessmen were shocked by the radical change of direction being demanded of them, but according to Alan Gear of the HDRA they were soon leading the way in devising efficient methods of growing potatoes organically.

Winds of Change

After more than half a century, during which the land has been progressively poisoned by agribusiness, it appears that the impending death of the soil may yet be averted. In fact, the winds of change may now be blowing in mother nature's favour, heralding the resurrection of the soil. The grounds for optimism can be assessed by studying the history of the organic movement in Britain, its changing fortunes and its spectacular growth in the past decade.

In 1946 Lady Eve Balfour founded the Soil Association to counter the neo-orthodoxy of post-war agriculture, which viewed pest and disease control as a continual battle against nature. Against the 'scientific' notion that agriculture was at war with nature, Lady Balfour stressed that true agriculture was at one with nature: 'the health of soil, plant, animal and man is one and indivisible'.[8] The Soil Association was dedicated to promoting a holistic vision of agriculture which, eschewing synthetic fertilizers and pesticides, sought to work in harmony with natural processes. In spite of its laudable aims, the organic movement remained marginalized during the first decades of its existence. Membership was low and very little organic produce found its way on to the market.

The marginal status of organic farmers in general and the Soil Association in particular during the early 1970s was summed up by Schumacher in *Small Is Beautiful*:

> For the last twenty-five years, a private, voluntary organization, the Soil Association, has been engaged in exploring the vital relationships between soil, plant, animal, and man; has undertaken and assisted relevant research; and has attempted to keep the public informed about developments in these fields. Neither the successful farmers nor the Soil Association have been able to attract official support or recognition. They have generally been dismissed as 'the muck and mystery people', because they are obviously outside the mainstream of modern technological progress. Their methods bear the mark of non-violence and humility towards the infinitely subtle system of natural harmony, and this stands in opposition to the life-style

*of the modern world. But if we now realize that the modern
life-style is putting us into mortal danger, we may find it in our
hearts to support and even join these pioneers rather than to
ignore or ridicule them.*

Throughout the sixties and seventies only the small number of
wholefood shops and other specialist outlets sold organic food
and even these were generally restricted to selling organic flour
and cereals. As Alan Gear remarked: 'If you wanted to eat organic fruit and vegetables you had little choice but to grow them
yourself!'[9] Many people chose to do so. By 1980 membership
of the Henry Doubleday Research Association, whose members
were principally small organic gardeners, had reached around six
thousand. By 1999 this had increased to 26,000. The first producer groups, the Organic Growers Association and British Organic
Farmers, were founded in the 1980s and it was during this decade
that supermarkets first started showing a serious interest in
organic produce, Safeway being the first to sell an organic range.

Yet it was from 1995 onwards, as consumers sought 'safe' food
in the wake of the BSE scare, that demand really began to rise.
By the end of 1997 retail sales of organic food in the UK were
increasing at more than 25 per cent a year. According to Alan
Gear, the Soil Association was 'overwhelmed' by the dramatic
renewal of interest in organic farming. Meanwhile the HDRA,
which had moved in 1984 from its one and a half acres in Essex
to a larger site near Coventry, found itself being courted by the
Ministry of Agriculture. It now has contracts from the government worth half a million pounds a year to research the most
efficient methods of converting test sites – which range in size
from twenty-five to five thousand acres – to organic farming. It's
a far cry from the days when Schumacher complained that the
organic movement was either ignored or ridiculed.

The HDRA also provides information to non-government organizations, such as church groups, in the developing world. Alan Gear is convinced that organic farming offers prospects for a 'huge increase in food production' in the developing countries.

Throughout Europe demand was even higher than in Britain, particularly in Scandinavia, where a fifth of all food consumption is from organically grown produce. In the United States demand is rising rapidly and entirely new chains of supermarkets selling all-organic produce are emerging.

Unfortunately, lack of government support for organic farming in Britain means that less than 1 per cent of agricultural land is farmed organically. This compares woefully with other European countries, such as Austria where 10 per cent of land is given over to organic production. As a result, more than 70 per cent of organic food bought in Britain is imported.

Reversing the Vandalism

The upsurge in demand for organic food will have far-reaching benefits. It will reverse the vandalism of industrial farming, which has systematically destroyed wildlife through pesticide poisoning and habitat destruction. The full extent of the damage inflicted by agribusiness between 1945 and 1984 was recorded in a report by the Nature Conservancy Council. It makes grim reading: 95 per cent of wildflower-rich meadows destroyed; up to half of ancient lowland woodlands destroyed; 80 per cent of lowland grasslands on chalk and limestone destroyed; more than half of lowland heaths destroyed; half of lowland fens destroyed or damaged; and half of upland grasslands, heaths and mires destroyed. Most damaging of all has been the loss of 140,000 miles of hedgerows.

The effect on wildlife of this wholesale destruction of their natural habitat has been catastrophic. In July 1998 a report by the British Trust for Conservation highlighted the dramatic decline in the number of farmland birds. Between 1972 and 1996 there had been a decline of 33 per cent in the numbers of blackbirds, 41 per cent in linnets, 52 per cent in song thrushes, and 62 per cent in bullfinches.

If, as present rates of growth suggest, 30 per cent of agricultural land in Europe is farmed organically by 2010, the resurrection of the soil will be accompanied by a restoration of lost habitats and consequently a revival of the species that depend on them. Not only does organic farming spurn the use of chemicals, it also relies on natural conservation features such as hedges, ponds and woodland. These are the breeding grounds for the natural predators that feed on insect pests. Furthermore, the organic standards insisted on by the Soil Association explicitly forbid farmers from the vandalism endemic in intensive farming methods. The Soil Association prohibits the ploughing of unimproved pastures and the trimming of hedges between the end of March and the beginning of September. It also forbids the ploughing of species-rich grassland and any drainage affecting wetlands of significant conservation value.

The benefits to bird populations of organic farming have been studied by researchers in both the United States and the United Kingdom. A study in Nebraska found that bird population densities on fields managed organically were six times those in chemically farmed fields. A similar study in the Midwest found that bird populations were between six and eight times higher on organic farms than on their intensively farmed neighbours. In the United Kingdom, the British Trust for Ornithology has conducted a number of studies which have found that birds do better on organic farms. In particular, endangered species such as the skylark show a noticeable improvement in chemical-free environments.

Assisting the Organic Revolution

Whether the criterion is human health or the health of the wider environment, the benefits of organic farming are beyond question. In order to maximize these benefits, positive action needs to be instigated so that the organic revolution can fulfil its potential to transform agriculture. Governments need to take proactive measures by levying taxes on chemical fertilizers and pesticides, using the extra revenue to promote the switch to organic production. There are plans for such a policy in the Netherlands, where the government is to increase VAT from 6 to 17.5 per cent on agrochemicals, spending the £50 million this will raise on environmentally friendly farming.

By contrast, support for the organic sector in Britain has been less than adequate. In October 1999 Richard Burge, chief executive of the Countryside Alliance, attacked the derisory sum being made available to farmers to go organic: 'The government's announcement of £10 million for organic farming is pathetic,' he said, adding that it 'is not enough to enable farms to achieve organic status'.

While the heavy-handed abuse of the land by the macro-politics of national governments and the European Union continues unabated, small communities are working for change in their local areas. Initiatives such as 'local food links' are helping to revitalize local economies. Their aim is to create direct links between local food producers and local consumers through the setting up of small-scale farmers' markets, the opening of farm shops, and the instigation of box schemes which deliver organic produce to the door. They also involve the publication of local food directories and, in some cases, the establishment of community orchards, food co-ops and other forms of community-supported agriculture.

Neither is this a purely rural phenomenon. The National Federation of City Farms is working successfully to bring organic farming to the heart of the city, transforming derelict urban land into city farms which improve the environment and the quality of life in the local community. There are now some seventy city farms and over five hundred community gardens, providing urban dwellers with an opportunity to get involved in producing food and improving the local environment. Under the slogan 'Plant a Seed and Grow a Community', the National Federation of City Farms provides sustainable community projects run by and for local people, encouraging wildlife and creating green oases in the midst of the concrete jungle.

The development of local initiatives is important for a variety of reasons beyond the need to overcome the inertia of central government. Above all they are needed as a response to the globalization of the food industry. Globalization means that more food is imported than ever before. This unnecessary and wasteful transportation over long distances of food which could be produced locally is environmentally harmful because the accumulation of 'food miles' increases pollution and necessitates excessive food processing and packaging. It also diverts money away from local economies, placing added strain on small rural communities. It wastes resources, degrades the environment and alienates people from the land.

In contrast, the development of sustainable local food economies, where food is produced, sold and consumed locally, brings a whole range of social, environmental and economic benefits. It creates a secure and loyal local market for local producers, re-establishing the close relationship between producer and consumer that is essential to social and economic cohesion. It will bolster local economies through increased local employment and will reduce transport, and consequently pollution, by offering a solution to the 'food miles' issue. In the words of Helena Norberg-Hodge, director of the International Society for Ecology and Culture: 'Promoting links between producers and consumers will not only give us healthier food and a cleaner environment, but will breathe new life into our communities – this is not just about agriculture – it is about the very fabric of our future.'

More than fifty years ago the wanton destruction of the soil was instigated by central planners. Today, the soil's resurrection is springing from the grass roots.

1 Schumacher, *Small Is Beautiful*, p. 96.
2 Ibid.
3 Ibid.
4 Susan Bayliss, Asda customer relations, letter to Joseph Pearce, 14 September 1999.
5 Shirley Kidd, Tesco customer service manager, letter to Joseph Pearce, 22 September 1999.
6 *Your Guide to Food You Can Trust*, an Iceland publication.
7 Norfolk Organic Gardeners *Newsletter*, August–October 1999, p. 22.
8 Gear, 'Organic and non-Organic Agriculture'.
9 Schumacher, *Small Is Beautiful*, p. 96.

14

Technology with a Human Face

If that which has been shaped by technology, and continues to be so shaped, looks sick, it might be wise to have a look at technology itself. If technology is felt to be becoming more and more inhuman, we might do well to consider whether it is possible to have something better – a technology with a human face.[1]

E.F. Schumacher

Apart from *Small Is Beautiful*, Schumacher's greatest contribution to the economic and meta-economic debate was probably his tireless promotion of intermediate technology. Inspired by the teaching of Gandhi, who proclaimed that what the poor of the world needed was not mass production but production by the masses, Schumacher sought to put technology at the service of the masses.

The system of mass production, as practised in the world's richest countries, requires a huge amount of capital investment and is dependent on high energy input. Since the poorest countries do not have the financial reserves to invest in these capital-intensive industries, their efforts to join the global economy have fuelled the large-scale borrowing that has created a crippling legacy of third world debt.

The world's poorest countries are caught in a debt trap that is keeping their people in poverty and preventing them from working their way into a sustainable future. In many cases, more is spent on paying or servicing debts than on providing essential services. Between 1993 and 1996 Zambia spent four times more on servicing its debt than on education. The government was forced to increase school fees, with the inevitable result that primary school enrolments in Zambia are now in decline. Rwanda spends more on debt than on health care and education combined. In fact, debt absorbs more than ten times its health budget.[2]

The extent to which the public finances of poor countries are shackled by debt can be seen by the percentage of government expenditure that goes on debt repayments. In Honduras debt accounts for a massive 60 per cent of total government expenditure; in Nicaragua it is 50 per cent; in Ethiopia and Zambia it is 25 per cent; in Tanzania 23 per cent; and in Niger it is 13 per cent. In each of these cases far more is spent on servicing debt than on primary education.[3]

The Burden of Debt

The debt problem in the poor countries has become particularly chronic over the past two decades. Many of the world's poorest countries are now so heavily burdened with debt that they will never be able to pay. These countries are effectively bankrupt. The International Monetary Fund (IMF) and World Bank have defined forty-one countries as having a serious debt problem under the Heavily Indebted Poor Country (HIPC) initiative. The total debt of these countries is over £100 billion (approximately $170 billion). The ability of these countries to service their debt, hopelessly inadequate in any case, is decreased further by recent falls in the world prices for the commodities on which they depend.

The debt crisis has meant that most governments of poor countries have had to take out new loans from the World Bank and the IMF simply to meet their payments on the original ones, and to cover the budget and trade deficits that the original debt has caused. It is a cruel and vicious circle. In political terms, the IMF and World Bank have been using their economic muscle to tighten their control on third world governments. Before these countries can gain access to aid they must have the explicit approval of the IMF and World Bank. Furthermore, loans from the IMF and the World Bank come with conditions set out under the terms of 'Structural Adjustment Programmes' (SAPs), which poor countries have been obliged to adopt regardless of the consequences for their own people. In practice these two institutions, unanswerable to any electorate, wield enormous power in many poor countries.

The Structural Adjustment Programmes demanded by the IMF and World Bank usually require drastic cuts in public spending on services such as health care and education. They also place pressure on governments to earn foreign exchange to service their debt through large-scale extractive projects such as mining or logging, which have detrimental effects ecologically. Thus the policies of the IMF and World Bank, imposed on debt-dependent poor governments, lead to the further impoverishing of both people and the environment. Apart from the harm that these Structural Adjustment Programmes inflict upon the hapless populations of the poorest countries, they also carry the stigma of neo-colonialism. They demand the liberalization of import controls and increased openness to foreign investment, which in practical terms means that these countries have to make themselves available for exploitation by the multinationals.

Neo-colonialism

Increasing opposition to this neo-colonialism led to violent protests at the meeting of the World Trade Organization in Seattle in November 1999 and at the meeting of the World Economic Forum in Davos, Switzerland in January 2001. The WTO, which evolved from the General Agreement on Tariffs and Trade (GATT), has been at the forefront of attempts by the rich nations of the world, and more specifically the multinationals, to impose their political and economic will on developing countries. This has had disastrous consequences.

Unable to see beyond the fundamental errors of conventional economic theory, the WTO has encouraged the introduction of intensive farming in third world countries. The effects have been even more devastating than the introduction of such methods under the Common Agricultural Policy in Europe. The intensification of agriculture is capital intensive and drastically reduces the number of people employed on the land. In poorer countries, where a high proportion of the population works on the land, it has forced millions of redundant farm workers to uproot from their villages and migrate to the cities. Throughout the developing world the major cities have exploded in size, with slum-infested suburbs accommodating the desperate millions forced to leave the land. Yet even the ugly surface does not reveal the full devastation. The invisible suffering beneath the surface is linked to the break-up of families, the desertion and pollution of the countryside, and the destruction of traditional cultures and the social stability they nurture.

The dangers were evident to Schumacher a quarter of a century ago: 'Rural unemployment produces mass-migration into cities, leading to a rate of urban growth which would tax the resources of even the richest societies. Rural unemployment becomes urban unemployment.'[4] Even today, when the problem is many times worse than it was when Schumacher's words were written, the economic 'experts' of the WTO, the IMF and the World Bank cannot bring themselves to question their own discredited dogmas.

It has been estimated that more than three billion people in the world still live on the land. If the WTO succeeds in intensifying agriculture to conform with economic dogma, two billion of these will become redundant. The effects are too horrifying to contemplate. These people will be forced to migrate, either to the already overcrowded cities of their own countries or, as the cities reach saturation point, to countries further afield. The result will be a disastrous destabilization of the world's population.

The policies of the WTO have exacerbated the problem even more by opening the developing world to the multinationals. Investment by multinational corporations in manufacturing plants in the third world's mega-cities accelerates the economic exodus from the land, destabilizing the social infrastructure of these countries still further. Again the problem was foreseen by Schumacher, who described the depopulation of the countryside and the consequent overcrowding of the cities as a process of mutual poisoning:

> As long as the development effort is concentrated mainly on the big cities, where it is easiest to establish new industries, to staff them with managers and men, and to find finance and markets to keep them going, the competition from these industries will further disrupt and destroy non-agricultural production in

the rest of the country, will cause additional unemployment outside, and will further accelerate the migration of destitute people into towns that cannot absorb them. The 'process of mutual poisoning' will not be halted.[5]

Not surprisingly, opposition has been growing. In India there have been demonstrations of up to a million people opposing the destruction of their rural communities, their culture and their traditions. In the Philippines several hundred thousand small farmers protested against the policies of the WTO, fearing the imminent destruction of their system of agriculture and their traditional way of life.

Vandana Shiva, an Indian philosopher and physicist who is director of the Research Foundation for Science, Technology and National Resource Policy, summed up the concerns of many in the developing world. In India, she said, global free trade 'will mean a further destruction of our communities, uprooting of millions of small peasants from the land, and their migration into the slums of overcrowded cities. GATT destroys the cultural diversity and social stability of our nation ... GATT, for us, implies recolonization.'[6]

Building a Sustainable Future

There are a number of initiatives being suggested to address the debt crisis, notably by organizations such as Oxfam. Ultimately, however, the long-term future of the world's poorest countries will depend on their ability to build a sustainable future through the use of intermediate technology. Instead of trying to join the globalist money-go-round which worships capital before labour and profits before people, the poorest countries should opt for a more appropriate future.

Most developing countries have plenty of labour and very little capital. Therefore, appropriate technology for these countries should be labour intensive. This does not mean that there is no place for machines, but that machines are to serve the abundant supply of labour, not replace it. 'I want the dumb millions of our land to be healthy and happy,' said Gandhi, 'and I want them to grow spiritually ... If we feel the need of machines, we certainly will have them. Every machine that helps every individual has a place, but there should be no place for machines that concentrate power in a few hands and turn the masses into mere machine minders, if indeed they do not make them unemployed.'[7]

To return to the words of Gandhi cited at the beginning of this chapter, the world's poorest countries should not be seeking mass production but production by the masses. This was discussed at length by Schumacher:

> *The system of* mass production, *based on sophisticated, highly capital-intensive, high energy-input dependent, and human labour-saving technology, presupposes that you are already rich, for a great deal of capital investment is needed to establish one single workplace. The system of* production by the masses *mobilises the priceless resources which are possessed by all human beings, their clever brains and skilful hands,* and supports them with first class tools. *The technology of* mass production *is inherently violent, ecologically damaging, self-defeating in terms of non-renewable resources, and stultifying for the human person. The technology of* production by the masses, *making use of the best of modern knowledge and experience, is conducive to decentralization, compatible with the laws of ecology, gentle in its use of scarce resources, and designed to serve the human person instead of making him the*

servant of machines. I have named it intermediate technology to signify that it is vastly superior to the primitive technology of bygone ages but at the same time much simpler, cheaper, and freer from the super-technology of the rich. One can also call it self-help technology, or democratic or people's technology – a technology to which everybody can gain admittance and which is not reserved to those already rich and powerful.[8]

It was necessary, Schumacher believed, that genuine development in the third world should bypass the big cities and concentrate instead on establishing an 'agro-industrial structure' in rural areas and small towns. This should comprise millions of small workplaces, each employing relatively few people in labour-intensive enterprises designed to meet local demands. The emphasis should not be, as conventional economists demand, on output per person but on providing work for people.

Schumacher stipulated four criteria which would be required for this 'agro-industrial structure' to be built successfully. First, the workplaces should be built where people were currently living and not in metropolitan areas, where they would only add to the mutual poisoning of rural and urban areas through migration. Second, the workplaces should be cheap enough to be established in large numbers without the need for intensive levels of capital investment. Third, production methods should be simple, minimizing the complexities created by the need for training, organization, sourcing raw materials, financing, marketing and so forth. Fourth, the production should be from local materials and mainly for local use.

These four requirements can only be met if development is devolved from central government and is carried out on a regional level, working within 'democracies of small areas' which are less subject to inefficient bureaucracy and the powerful vested interests that hold sway in macro-democracies.

Home-comers

Having made the distinction between intermediate technology and its capital-intensive counterpart, Schumacher discussed the essential philosophical difference between the proponents of each. Those who advocated the application of intermediate technology were, according to Schumacher, 'home-comers' seeking a more peaceful lifestyle and a 'return to certain basic truths about man and his world'. John Seymour, the doyen of the self-sufficiency movement, called such people 'drop-ins' – as distinct from the sixties 'drop-outs' – who desired to drop in to a healthier, gentler and more sustainable lifestyle. On the other hand, Schumacher described those who advocated capital-intensive technology as 'the people of the forward stampede'. For these people, the future is a race with the devil, technology always managing to stay one step ahead of the problems it causes.

Schumacher singled out Dr Sicco Mansholt, whose plan for agriculture (see chapter 11) had caused such widespread damage throughout Europe, as a typical representative of the 'forward stampede'. 'More, further, quicker, richer are the watchwords of present-day society', said Mansholt approvingly. His was the authentic voice of the forward stampede. 'More, further, quicker, richer', coupled with 'New!' and 'Now!', were the battle cries of the big-is-best brigade who, like the legendary Light Brigade would charge headlong into the valley of death because 'someone had blundered'.

Set against this technological feeding frenzy, financed by international loan-sharks, there was the 'still, small voice' of the home-comers, who had the courage to say no to the new and the now. 'And what about the other side?' asked Schumacher. 'This is made up of people who are deeply convinced that technological development has taken a wrong turn and needs to be redirected.'

The term 'home-comer' has, of course, a religious connotation. For it takes a good deal of courage to say 'no' to the fashions and fascinations of the age and to question the presuppositions of a civilization which appears destined to conquer the whole world; the requisite strength can be derived only from deep convictions ... The genuine 'home-comer' ... has the most exalted text, nothing less than the Gospels. For him, there could not be a more concise statement of his situation, of our situation, than the parable of the prodigal son. Strange to say, the Sermon on the Mount gives pretty precise instructions on how to construct an outlook that could lead to an Economics of Survival.

– How blessed are those who know that they are poor;
the Kingdom of Heaven is theirs.
– How blessed are the sorrowful;
they shall find consolation.
– How blessed are those of a gentle spirit;
they shall have the earth for their possession.
– How blessed are those who hunger and thirst to see right
*   prevail;*
they shall be satisfied.
– How blessed are the peacemakers;
God shall call them his sons.

It may seem daring to connect these beatitudes with matters of technology and economics. But may it not be that we are in trouble precisely because we have failed for so long to make this connection? It is not difficult to discern what these beatitudes may mean for us today:

— We are poor, not demigods.
— We have plenty to be sorrowful about, and are not emerging into a golden age.
— We need a gentle approach, a non-violent spirit, and small is beautiful.
— We must concern ourselves with justice and see right prevail.
— And all this, only this, can enable us to become peacemakers.[9]

The spirit of these economic beatitudes was also central to the vision of Mahatma Gandhi. Like Schumacher, Gandhi knew that economics and technology are worthless if they fail to recognize the spiritual truth at the heart of humanity. 'There must be recognition of the existence of the soul apart from the body,' said Gandhi, 'and of its permanent nature, and this recognition must amount to a living faith; and, in the last resort, non-violence does not avail those who do not possess a living faith in the God of Love.'[10]

In practical terms, this recognition required intermediate technology – technology with a human face. As Schumacher wrote:

I have no doubt that it is possible to give a new direction to technological development, a direction that shall lead it back to the real needs of man, and that also means: to the actual size of man. Man is small, and, therefore, small is beautiful. To go for giantism is to go for self-destruction. And what is the cost of a reorientation? We might remind ourselves that to calculate the cost of survival is perverse. No doubt, a price has to be paid for anything worth while: to redirect technology so that it serves man instead of destroying him requires primarily an effort of the imagination and an abandonment of fear.[11]

Those with imagination who had abandoned fear were the home-comers, who, with their gentle approach and non-violent spirit, had turned their back on the forward stampede. Seeking a simpler way that sought the beautiful in the small, they were secure in the sublime wisdom that only the gentle could inherit the earth because the hard-hearted, the proud and the violent could succeed only in destroying it.

1 Schumacher, *Small Is Beautiful*, p. 122.
2 Oxfam International, *Debt and Education*, 1999.
3 Ibid.
4 Schumacher, *Small Is Beautiful*, p. 144.
5 Ibid.
6 Quoted in Goldsmith, *The Trap*, p. 32.
7 Quoted in Schumacher, *Small Is Beautiful*, pp. 27–8.
8 Schumacher, *Small Is Beautiful*, p. 122.
9 Ibid., pp. 130–31.
10 Quoted in Schumacher, *Small Is Beautiful*, p. 32.
11 Schumacher, *Small Is Beautiful*, p. 133.

15

Green Technology

Although we are in possession of all requisite knowledge, it still requires a systematic, creative effort to bring this technology into active existence and make it generally visible and available. It is my experience that it is rather more difficult to recapture directness and simplicity than to advance in the direction of ever more sophistication and complexity. Any third-rate engineer or researcher can increase complexity; but it takes a certain flair of real insight to make things simple. And this insight does not come easily to people who have allowed themselves to become alienated from real, productive work and from the self-balancing system of nature, which never fails to recognize measure and limitation. Any activity which fails to recognize a self-limiting principle is of the devil.[1]

E.F. Schumacher

'World poverty is primarily a problem of two million villages,' wrote Schumacher, 'and thus a problem of two thousand million villagers … Unless life in the hinterland can be made tolerable, the problem of world poverty is insoluble and will inevitably get worse.'[2] Since the problem is principally rural, its solution cannot be found in the cities of the poor countries. Still less can it be imposed by the financial, commercial and political elites in the cities of the rich countries. Schumacher again:

> *The aid-givers – rich, educated, town-based – know how to do things in their own way; but do they know how to assist self-help among two million villages, among two thousand million villagers – poor, uneducated, country-based? They know how to do a few big things in big towns; but do they know how to do thousands of small things in rural areas? They know how to do things with lots of capital; but do they know how to do them with lots of labour…?*[3]

In fact, many of the problems faced by the rural poor are the direct or indirect result of the short-sighted policies imposed by the urban rich. In slavishly following the dogmas of conventional economics, the urban-based elites in the developing world, actively coerced and encouraged by multinationals, financiers and the governments of rich nations, have created many new problems and aggravated existing ones. Efforts at artificial grafting operations, carried out by foreign technicians under the patronage of foreign multinationals and indigenous elites that have lost contact with the aspirations of ordinary people, have been ineffective at best, disastrous at worst. The only solution is a dissolution of central planning and the resolution of problems at a local and regional level.

It was Schumacher's belief that development could only be effective if it reached down to, and sprang up from, the heartland of world poverty, the two million villages. 'If the disintegration of rural life continues, there is no way out – no matter how much money is being spent. But if the rural people of the developing countries are helped to help themselves, I have no doubt that a genuine development will ensue, without vast shanty towns and misery belts around every big city...'[4]

Yet the problem of urban centralization is not restricted to the developing countries. On the contrary it is worse, in many respects, in the richest countries. The problem, and its destructive effects, is a global phenomenon:

> The all-pervading disease of the modern world is the total imbalance between city and countryside, an imbalance in terms of wealth, power, culture, attraction, and hope. The former has become over-extended and the latter has atrophied. The city has become the universal magnet, while rural life has lost its savour. Yet it remains an unalterable truth that ... the health of the cities depends on the health of the rural areas. The cities, with all their wealth, are merely secondary producers, while primary production, the precondition of all economic life, takes place in the countryside. The prevailing lack of balance ... today threatens all countries throughout the world, the rich even more than the poor. To restore a proper balance between city and rural life is perhaps the greatest task in front of modern man.[5]

Technology As If People Mattered

In rich and poor countries alike, the challenge is to raise the whole level of rural life, 'and this requires the development of an agro-industrial culture, so that each district, each community, can offer a colourful variety of occupations to its members'.[6] In practical terms this will require the application of appropriate technology throughout the world, in the rich countries as in the poor. Instead of the macro-technologies imposed on humanity by the international powers, it heralds the dawn of new technologies designed to enable individuals, small businesses and small communities to help themselves. It is technology as if people mattered.

This people-friendly technology has the added advantage of being environmentally friendly. An obvious example is the development of renewable energy sources and energy-conservation technology. Paradoxically, the pioneers of green energy have included some of the largest utility companies in the United States. Pacific Gas and Electric, based in California, has developed a run-of-the-mill, mid-priced house that needs neither heating nor cooling equipment. It includes new insulation methods; windows which admit light but which insulate from heat; lighting systems which reduce electricity consumption by 80 to 90 per cent; and new air-conditioning systems which reduce the consumption of electricity by more than 90 per cent.[7] It is estimated that it will use only a fifth of the energy prescribed by the most rigorous US building standards. Furthermore, if the technology were widely adopted, it would actually cost $1,800 less to build than a similar-sized energy-guzzling house.

Pacific Gas and Electric has employed this technology in its own offices, reducing electricity consumption by 75 per cent. The capital investment required if the whole of the United States were to convert to these new systems has been estimated at about $200 billion. Yet the annual saving would be in the order of $100 to $130 billion, a spectacular rate of return.[8]

Detailed studies have shown that similar savings could be made by introducing the technology in Europe. It has been estimated that electricity consumption could be reduced by 50 per cent in Sweden and possibly as much as 75 per cent in Denmark. In Germany it may be possible to save up to 80 per cent of electricity consumed by private households. Furthermore, all these savings have been shown to be cost-effective.[9]

Renewable Energy

Parallel with the development of technology designed to conserve energy has been research into the application of renewable energy sources. This has particular relevance to the developing world because the construction of quite small wind turbines could provide electricity for isolated villages, increasing the ability of rural areas to help themselves while decreasing the need for large and polluting fossil-fuel power stations that accelerate the process of urbanization.

A good example of the practical application of appropriate technology in the developing world has been the widespread construction of improved water mills in Nepal.

Like most developing countries, Nepal's economy is dependent on agriculture. According to figures published in the early 1990s, agriculture provides more than 68 per cent of Nepal's GDP and 75 per cent of its exports. Farming provides a livelihood for 94 per cent of the population. The country's numerous rivers and its mountainous terrain provides an enormous potential for the development of hydro-electric power. This potential has been tapped by the Nepalese for centuries through the construction of horizontal water wheels, traditionally known as *ghattas*. Today there are estimated to be around 25,000 of these traditional *ghattas* in operation throughout the country. Typically, there are one or two *ghattas* in every mountain village.

Traditional *ghattas*, which only generate about 1 horsepower, are normally used to grind grain into flour. Recently, however, this environmentally benign power source has benefited from appropriate technological innovation. Rather than radically altering the traditional design through the introduction of crossflow turbines which would require large capital outlay beyond the means of the local communities, these innovations sought small, simple improvements upon the basic *ghatta*. Local artisans, working in co-operation with technology agencies, have succeeded in upgrading mill technology in a way which is affordable even for the poorest communities. The improved *ghattas*, which have increased the power output of each mill from one horsepower to three horsepower or more, are constructed from local materials and can be produced by village craftsmen. Furthermore, the structural conversion of old traditional *ghattas* to the new improved version can be carried out by local labour.

The increased power output of the improved *ghattas* provide a cheap and reliable source of energy which is helping to revitalize the rural economy. These mills can drive small machines in local workshops, or can be used to pump irrigation water to surrounding crops.[10]

The application of appropriate technology and renewable energy systems is equally beneficial to the healthy development of rural areas in rich countries. In August 1999 the most powerful wind turbine in the United Kingdom was erected in Swaffham, a small Norfolk market town. It provides electricity for half the town's population of six thousand and will prevent the emission of 3,000 tonnes of carbon dioxide, 39 tonnes of sulphur dioxide and 3 tonnes of nitrogen oxides each year, as well as tonnes of ash and slag waste. Within five months of beginning operation it had generated an equivalent amount of energy to that used in its construction, its transport to the site and its installation.[11]

187

Ecotech

The wind turbine in Swaffham was constructed on the site of the EcoTech Discovery Centre, opened four months earlier on a brownfield site on the outskirts of the town. Described as an 'environmental education centre', its purpose is 'to change the way people think about the environment'.[12] At the heart of the project is the desire to heighten public awareness of energy saving and sustainable development. The building has a Norwegian spruce frame, harvested from sustainable sources, and all the paint used on the building is organic. It has a massive glazed southern front which transmits solar energy deep into the building. The northern side is heavily insulated with organic materials made from recycled newspapers to prevent heat loss, while shading on the southern front, using automatic blinds and natural ventilation, prevents overheating in summer. In the winter, thinnings from nearby Thetford Forest provide green heating and the centre is powered by the adjacent wind turbine.

The centre seeks to point to viable and sustainable solutions and to act as a focus for practical action in the community. It offers constructive advice on sensible water usage and energy conservation, as well as ways in which individuals can improve the environment for plants and animals. There are also a number of innovative new products on display, such as a fleece jacket made from recycled plastic bottles.

Part of the land surrounding the EcoTech Centre is being developed by the EcoTech Garden Group, which aims to train local people in all aspects of organic growing. As well as teaching people to grow fruit and vegetables without recourse to chemical spraying and other damaging inputs, the Garden Group offers instruction in a variety of traditional countryside crafts, such as willow weaving, hedging, conservation techniques, pruning and permaculture. The garden, which provides all the organic vegetables on sale at the Centre's restaurant, is being expanded to include a 'Norfolk orchard' which will have forty fruit trees, each a different local variety.

EcoTech is at the hub of efforts to promote rural regeneration. It has a learning centre offering free classes for people living locally. Working closely with the local district council, EcoTech is at the centre of a scheme to promote small businesses involved in environmentally friendly products and processes. The first two businesses to be located at the EcoTech Centre are Anglia Woodnet, which provides woodland management advice and is working on a new charcoal product from local woodlands, and Crop Enhancement Systems, which advises businesses on how best to adopt and promote the environmentally friendly use of resources.

Murree Groom, director of Crop Enhancement Systems, explains that CES promotes an antibody diagnostic system to test for pesticides, industrial pollutants, plant toxins and fungi. The test kits can also be used to detect GM protein inserts in maize or pesticide levels in boreholes. Groom hopes that his diagnostic kits will be used in children's education and will be adopted by the national curriculum to encourage environmental awareness in the young. The quick-sticks in his kits could be used by school field trips to test for pollutants in water and the soil.

'Only recently has science discovered the complex eco-balance at work in agriculture,' says Groom. 'As organic farming develops it needs to evolve into a very sophisticated farming methodology using the abundance of ecosystem knowledge. This should facilitate a return to traditional techniques.' A vision of traditional farming ably assisted by green technology is at the heart of Murree Groom's hopes for the future.[13]

A similar initiative to EcoTech has been taken elsewhere in Norfolk by the National Trust. A new £1 million environmental system was opened in May 1999 on the coast at Brancaster. It features the latest sustainable energy technology, including a geothermal energy recovery system, photothermal and photovoltaic panels and a wind generator. All the materials used in the renovation of the building, the seventeenth-century Dial House, were assessed for their environmental friendliness by the National Trust and include recycled materials. The education programme on offer at the centre is closely linked to the national curriculum.[14]

The scheme at Brancaster is indicative of a major shift of emphasis by the National Trust in the direction of green technology. The Trust has called for a reduction in the use of fossil fuels and has actively started to promote environmentally benign energy. It is responding to the extensive damage caused to its land and buildings, by acid rain in the Pennines and the Welsh uplands, by the release of nitrogen through the burning of fossil fuels in its wetland and heathland habitats, and by rising sea levels causing erosion and flooding along its coastal sites. The Trust is also reviewing its own energy use in all property management plans. It is developing alternative transport for staff and visitors and is installing 18,500 low-energy light bulbs in all properties.

Apart from its pioneering scheme at Brancaster, the Trust has installed hydropower at Houghton Mill in Cambridge, geothermal power in Botallack in Cornwall and a combined solar, hydro and wood-powered system at Gibson Mill in Yorkshire, and is exploring the use of small-scale wind-powered generators to provide power locally for Trust properties. Echoing Schumacher's words, the Trust has called for the development of local initiatives as the key to revitalizing rural communities.[15]

Blazing a Trail

Although the new initiatives by EcoTech and the National Trust are encouraging, one particular sustainable technology project has been blazing a trail for almost thirty years. Back in the early seventies, a group of young idealists colonized a derelict slate quarry in mid-Wales. Their aim was to live sustainably through the use of the emerging green technologies. A few years later the group felt sufficiently established and confident to open its doors to the public. So, in 1975, the Centre for Alternative Technology (CAT) was born. Its purpose was 'to develop and prove, by a positive living example, new technologies which would provide practical solutions to the problems that are worrying the world's ecologists'.

According to Jacinta MacDermot of CAT's information department, the Centre for Alternative Technology

> concentrates on the domestic application of alternative technologies. For most people, stand-alone renewable energy electricity systems are not going to be appropriate (except in the case of solar water heating) though more and more people are now able to support renewables through conventional electricity suppliers ... Much of the work we do is to provide people with the information they need to live more sustainably in other ways – through consumer choice of low impact materials, energy efficiency, organic growing etc.[16]

A welcome financial ally of those seeking sustainable technology has emerged in the form of the Triodos Bank. Established in the Netherlands in 1980, Triodos has the specific objective of providing banking services solely for enterprises with environmental objectives, such as renewable energy, organic agriculture and fair trade. After fifteen years in which it played a key role in financing organic agriculture in the Netherlands, it established itself in Britain in 1995. Since then it has helped finance a range of green initiatives. It has helped many farmers to convert from chemical to organic agriculture and it provided 80 per cent of the finances for the wind turbine in Swaffham. Other projects which have benefited from funding by the Triodos Bank include whole-food shops, producers' co-operatives, and several renewable energy projects such as wind farms and small-scale wind and solar energy systems.

In the years since *Small Is Beautiful* was first published, Schumacher's call for appropriate or intermediate technology has been answered by an ever-increasing number of people. The emergence of new technology with a human face gives hope to those who seek a sustainable future. Yet the hope should not give way to naive optimism. Science, or more correctly scientism, is still put to the service of the giantism that is laying waste to our earth. If, on the other hand, science were put in the service of green technology it would become a tool for humanity's survival, not a weapon for its destruction. Science must overcome scientism, its worship of itself, and become the meta-science that will cease to be life-threatening. Science is not above morality. It should not be the master of humanity but its faithful servant.

1 Schumacher, *Small Is Beautiful*, p. 129.
2 Ibid., p. 162.
3 Ibid., p. 164.
4 Ibid., p. 171.
5 Ibid., p. 170.
6 Ibid., p. 171.

7 Goldsmith, *The Trap*, pp. 141–2.

8 Ibid., p. 142.

9 Ibid., pp. 142–3.

10 Matthew S. Gamser, Helen Appleton & Nicola Carter (eds.), *Tinker, Tiller, Technical Change*, London: Intermediate Technology Publications, 1990, pp. 136–45.

11 *Breckland Voice*, Autumn 1999, pp. 10–11.

12 EcoTech press release, April 1999.

13 Murree Groom, interview with Joseph Pearce, 27 September 1999.

14 *National Trust Magazine*, Autumn 1999.

15 Ibid.

16 Jacinta MacDermot, letter to Joseph Pearce, 2 November 1999.

PART 5

Living Legacy

16

Co-operate and Prosper

The law, therefore, should favour ownership and its policy should be to induce as many people as possible to become owners. Many excellent results will follow from this; and first of all, property will certainly become more equitably divided ... If workpeople can be encouraged to look forward to obtaining a share in the land, the result will be that the gulf between vast wealth and deep poverty will be bridged over, and the two orders will be brought nearer together.[1]

Leo XIII

Pope Leo XIII's call for widely distributed ownership was one of the major influences on Schumacher's vision for a sustainable future. Beginning as a Marxist, Schumacher passed through a period of disillusionment and Buddhist enlightenment that prompted his search for realistic and radical alternatives to the way the world is run. 'He embarked upon an enormous course of reading,' says Christopher Derrick, a writer who befriended Schumacher during the final years of his life. 'Then somebody said you should read the social encyclicals of the Popes of Rome ... He did so and was absolutely staggered. He said, "Here were these celibates living in an ivory tower ... why can they talk so much sense when everyone else talks nonsense"...'[2]

The importance of these encyclicals to Schumacher's final distillation of the ideas which came to maturity in *Small Is Beautiful* should not be understated. On 15 May 1961 Pope John XXIII published *Mater et Magistra* (*Mother and Teacher*), his first social encyclical. In the opening paragraphs the Pope restated the Church's right to teach on matters of justice in society. He devoted the whole of the first part to emphasizing that he adhered faithfully to the social teaching of his predecessors, Leo XIII, Pius XI and Pius XII. Pope John drew attention to the teaching of Pius XI that the wage contract 'should, when possible, be modified somewhat by a clear reference to the right of the wage-earner to share in the profits, and, indeed, to sharing, as appropriate, in decision-making in his place of work'.

Reinforcing his predecessor's teaching, Pope John wrote that 'it is our conviction that the workers should make it their aim to be involved in the organized life of the firm by which they are employed and in which they work'. These principles animated the efforts of many Christians working for social justice throughout the 1960s. Perhaps the most dramatic fruition of papal teaching was in the Mondragon region of Spain where, inspired by the efforts of a campaigning priest, whole sections of industry became successful producers' co-operatives which still flourish today.

The Heart of Economic Life

The social teaching of the Catholic Church, summarized in the documents of the Second Vatican Council, centres on the principle that business enterprises are not primarily units of production but places where 'persons ... associate together, that is, men who are free and autonomous, created in the image of God'. Such a view delighted Schumacher since it placed humanity at the heart of economic life. The practical principle which sprang logically and inevitably from this was that economic activity must become 'user friendly'. Economics should be carried out on a human scale so that people could express themselves in a natural environment free from the alienation inherent in macro-economic enterprises. This was radical in the true sense, breaking the mould of economic convention so that life could return to the roots of human need and aspiration.

In his call for widely distributed ownership, the Pope would have found a staunch ally in Alexander Solzhenitsyn. 'There can be no independent citizen without private property,' Solzhenitsyn wrote in *Rebuilding Russia*. 'The truth is that ownership of modest amounts of property which does not oppress others must be seen as an integral component of personality, and as a factor contributing to its stability.'[3] With this central principle in mind, Solzhenitsyn advocated widespread land redistribution as a means of revitalizing post-communist Russia: 'Land embodies moral as well as economic values for human beings.'[4] Rural regeneration, in the wake of the destruction wrought by years of enforced collective farming, required the private ownership of land. 'To deny private ownership of land to the village is to finish it off for ever.' Yet such ownership must be introduced with caution to ensure that land was sold to small farmers, 'not to major speculators or to surrogates through joint-stock companies'.[5] The acreage of land purchases should be restricted in size, and should 'benefit from a multi-year repayment plan, as well as preferential tax treatment'.[6]

Solzhenitsyn's vision, intended as a means of revitalizing Russia, is equally applicable throughout the rest of the world.

Rebuilding Russia deserves to stand beside *Small Is Beautiful* as a permanent monument to the concepts of smallness, subsidiarity and economic sanity. The remarkable affinity between Solzhenitsyn and Schumacher was in further evidence in the former's call for the principle of widely distributed ownership to be extended to capital as well as to land:

> *healthy private initiative must be given wide latitude, and small private enterprise of every type must be encouraged and protected, since they are what will ensure the most rapid flowering of every locality. At the same time there should be firm legal limits to the unchecked concentration of capital; no monopolies should be permitted to form in any sector, and no enterprise should be in control of any other.*[7]

At this point, opponents of the redistribution of productive property to a larger number of people will raise the issue of the economies of scale. Such redistribution of ownership may be possible with regard to agricultural land, they will argue, but it is not possible with regard to industrial capital. It is all very well to encourage small businesses and even to discourage monopolies, but economies of scale will always dictate that many companies remain large in size and multinational in scope. If this is so, where does it leave the individual's right to a share in ownership? Is such a right rendered null and void by the economies of scale? Is it fine in principle but unworkable in practice?

Such questions obscure the issue. They put secondary considerations before primary realities. If a right exists it should not be sacrificed for an 'economy', especially one which worships giantism for its own sake. Furthermore, if a principle is fine it should not be dismissed as unworkable but should be made as workable as practically possible. We may not live in an ideal world but that should not prevent us striving to make our world as close to the ideal as possible.

How then, in the face of seemingly insurmountable obstacles such as the economies of scale, can the ownership of land and capital be extended to as many people as possible? This is the key question.

There are three practical areas in which land and capital can be brought closer to a far greater number of people. First is the active encouragement of small businesses through the implementation of policies designed to protect them from the encroachments of their larger rivals. Second is the implementation of Schumacher's Theory of Large-Scale Organization, which calls for the practical application of 'smallness within bigness'. Third is the widespread establishment of producers' co-operatives which ensure the right to land and capital through mutual ownership. The first two have been discussed already in chapter 7, while this chapter and the next will focus on the practical application and proven success of producers' co-operatives.

The Scott Bader Commonwealth

In 1967 Schumacher became a trustee of the Scott Bader Commonwealth, a producers' co-operative established in 1951 when its owner, Ernest Bader, transferred ownership to his workforce. Bader, a Quaker, believed that establishing co-operative ownership was an expression of Christian social principles in practice. To the surprise of many sceptics, who doubted whether such an enterprise could survive in a capitalist economy, the Scott Bader Commonwealth prospered. It became a pathfinder in polymer technology and a model of good labour relations at a time of considerable labour unrest throughout the rest of industry.

The history of this pioneering company serves as a shining example of what can be achieved through resilient faith and a stubborn determination to succeed in a hostile environment. Ernest Bader founded the Scott Bader Co. Ltd in 1920 when he was thirty years old. Thirty-one years later he had built the enterprise into a prosperous medium-sized business employing 161 people, with an annual turnover of £625,000 and net profits exceeding £72,000. By this time, Scott Bader had established a reputation as a leading producer of polyester resins, alkyds, polymers and plasticizers.

Ernest Bader had made a considerable fortune and could have been forgiven for resting on his laurels. He was not, however, an ordinary employer motivated solely by the desire for self-enrichment. As a young man he had been prompted to establish his own company because of a deep dissatisfaction with the prospect of remaining a propertyless employee for the rest of his life. He had resented the concept of a 'labour market' and a 'wages system', and felt keenly the injustice of capital employing people, instead of people employing capital. Even as a wealthy employer, Bader never lost sight of the vision of his youth. 'I realized that – as years ago when I took the plunge and ceased to be an employee – I was up against the capitalist philosophy of dividing people into the managed on the one hand, and those that manage on the other. The real obstacle, however, was Company Law, with its provisions for dictatorial powers of shareholders and the hierarchy of management they control.'[8]

In spite of these obstacles he was determined to introduce 'revolutionary changes' to the structure of his company 'based on a philosophy which attempts to fit industry to human needs'. The changes would require the resolution of two problems. First there was the challenge of combining 'a maximum sense of freedom, happiness and human dignity in our firm without loss of profitability'. Second was the need 'to do this by ways and means that could be generally acceptable to the private sector of industry'.[9]

Bader believed that the desire to maximize freedom, happiness and human dignity was not fulfilled by mere profit-sharing, which he had always practised. A more radical response was needed. In 1951 he set up the Scott Bader Commonwealth, transferring 90 per cent of his ownership of the company to his former employees. Twelve years later he transferred the remaining 10 per cent.

From the outset, the Scott Bader Commonwealth embodied a spirit of self-limitation. Its constitution stipulated that it should remain a company of limited size, employing no more than 350 people or thereabouts. This ensured that its members would continue to work within a human-scale enterprise. If circumstances appeared to dictate that growth was necessary beyond this self-imposed limit, the growth should be met by helping to set up new, complementary but fully independent units organized along similar lines to the Scott Bader Commonwealth. The constitution also stipulated that remuneration for work within the organization should not vary between the lowest and highest paid beyond a ratio of 1:7, before tax.

Since members of the Commonwealth would be partners and not employees they could not be dismissed by their co-partners for any reason other than gross personal misconduct. Similarly, the board of directors would be answerable to the Commonwealth, which would have the power to confirm or withdraw the appointment of directors and to set their level of remuneration. Up to 40 per cent of the net profits could be appropriated by the Commonwealth each year, half of which would be paid out to its members as bonuses and the other half donated for charitable purposes outside the Scott Bader organization. Finally, none of Scott Bader's products were to be sold to customers who were known to use them for war-related purposes.

Not surprisingly, many conventional economists predicted that these revolutionary changes would spell the imminent demise of Ernest Bader's company. It was widely believed that a company owned by its workforce could not possibly survive in a highly competitive capitalist market. In giving his company away, many felt that Bader had lost his senses as well as his property.

Yet predictions of Scott Bader's imminent demise were not only premature but were soon confounded as it went from strength to strength. Between 1951 and 1971, as Schumacher reported in *Small Is Beautiful*, sales increased from £625,000 to £5 million per annum and net annual profits from £72,000 to nearly £300,000. The number of Commonwealth members had increased from 161 to 379 and bonuses amounting to over £150,000 had been distributed to members, with an equal amount going to charity. Over the years substantial amounts of money have been allocated to a wide range of charitable projects, including the provision of water to rural villages in Africa and India, health care clinics in South America and many projects for the homeless in Britain.

Twenty years after he had given his company away, Ernest Bader looked with satisfaction at the Commonwealth's success:

> … the experience gained during many years of effort to establish the Christian way of life in our business has been a great encouragement; it has brought us good results in our relations with one another, as well as in the quality and quantity of our production.

Now we wish to press on and consummate what we have so far achieved, making a concrete contribution towards a better society in the service of God and our fellow men.[10]

The Scott Bader Commonwealth has continued to prosper in the past thirty years. In 1975 it received the Queen's Award to Industry for technical innovation in surface coatings. In the following year, when the passing of the Common Ownership Act recognized common ownership companies in law, the first certificate was awarded to Scott Bader.

In 1978 and 1982, with the economy in recession, voluntary redundancies were required for the first time. During this period many of Scott Bader's competitors were disappearing. There was much 'consolidation', small companies being bought out, merged and internationalized. The market was becoming increasingly dominated by a handful of multinational giants. Scott Bader survived because its ownership structure meant that it was beyond the reach of corporate takeover. It had no shareholders demanding short-term profits and could concentrate on longer-term objectives.

It was felt at this time, says Scott Bader company secretary Andrew Gunn, that there was a need to 'cushion ourselves' and to diversify. There were 'too many fingers in one pie'.[11] In practical terms this made it necessary to reduce dependence on the UK economy and to increase exports. The Commonwealth bounced back and from 1985 it has prospered as never before. In 1999 it had a turnover of £100 million and net profits in excess of £3 million. It now has subsidiaries in France, Sweden, Dubai, South Africa, the United States and the Czech Republic.

Facing New Challenges

Scott Bader's new multinational status has forced its members to face up to a dilemma touching the ethical foundation of the Commonwealth's existence. Those employed in the foreign subsidiaries are not Commonwealth members but employees, a situation which falls short of the high ideals that inspired Scott Bader's foundation. Andrew Gunn and his colleagues Denise Sayer and Stuart Reeves are candid in their discussion of the problems surrounding overseas expansion and the challenge it presents. They have struggled to persuade those employed in the French subsidiary of the benefits of common ownership but have had little success.

'The issue of extending common ownership across the channel to France has been around for at least ten years,' says Gunn, adding that resistance to change is rooted in cultural differences. It is neither desirable nor possible to force the structure of the Scott Bader Commonwealth too rigidly on those with different cultural aspirations. 'We can't have the same Commonwealth structure in Dubai, in South Africa or in France,' says Sayer, though she adds that these cultural differences should not be used as an excuse for inaction. Gunn and Sayer remain determined that all aspects of the Commonwealth's activities should live up to the principles that inspired its foundation. Any difficulties must eventually be overcome. The challenge is to create a federation of similar commonwealths, taking into account cultural differences. This should be consistent with the principle of subsidiarity, decentralizing power to the different subsidiaries while retaining a co-ordinating body to oversee international co-operation.

Andrew Gunn insists that the spiritual aspects of Ernest Bader's vision, such as the belief that all people are 'born equal before God', are as important as ever to the Commonwealth. Denise Sayer stresses that these ethical principles are an integral part of the education programme which all new members of the Commonwealth undergo. During their first six months of probationary membership, new members attend workshops in which 'the history, the philosophy and the ways of working of the Commonwealth are explained to them in quite a lot of depth'. Although people can choose not to be members, remaining merely as employees, more than three-quarters opt for membership – 302 out of a total UK workforce of 380 are members of the Commonwealth. All members have one vote at the quarterly general meetings regardless of their position within the company.

In a small booklet entitled *Towards a Better Future*, 'the principles and commitments of Scott Bader companies worldwide' are stated clearly. These include the principle of 'sustaining peaceful development':

> *Scott Bader Companies are particularly aware of the wider world and our duty to actively promote sustainable peaceful development in all our activities. We limit our products to those beneficial to the community and we exclude products for the specific purpose of manufacturing weapons of war.*
>
> *Scott Bader Companies also exclude products which damage the natural environment and seek to use resources as effectively as possible through flexible waste conscious, creative working practices.*
>
> *We believe in sharing with the wider community, both locally and globally. We distribute a significant proportion of our profits by making donations to charities which support the economic and social development of those less fortunate.*

As well as villages in the developing world and larger projects to help the homeless in Britain, the local area around the small Northamptonshire village where Scott Bader is based is a regular beneficiary of the company's charitable contributions. The Commonwealth funded the building of the village hall and a birdwatching site in the neighbouring valley. It actively promotes charitable awareness among its members, matching any sum of money they raise for local charities. According to Andrew Gunn, Scott Bader fosters an 'environment in which these outlooks are valued and encouraged'.

Putting Theory Into Practice

Gunn insists that Scott Bader is ultimately about putting theory into practice. The theory is 'wonderful on paper but it is a struggle to make it work … It is like the Kingdom of Heaven. You can't just step into it. You have to work towards it.' Many people join the Commonwealth expecting instant utopia and are almost as instantly disappointed. They pass from initial euphoria to a disillusioned depression because the theory is not put perfectly into practice. Gunn likens Scott Bader's position to a crusade or a quest for the Holy Grail. 'It is a struggle to make the practice measure up to the theory … It is a vision. We are on the road.' His colleague Stuart Reeves also sees parallels with the Christian struggle:

> I do liken it to the spiritual journey of a Christian towards the Kingdom of God. He sees the ideal and he journeys towards it. He doesn't always get it right. It is the 'Pilgrim's Progress'. And in the same way that people who go to church are sometimes scorned as being a rotten lot who fail to live up to their principles, we are sometimes scorned for failing to live up to the

*principles of the Commonwealth. It is human nature or origi-
nal sin or whatever you want to call it. It is the struggle to reach
perfection.*[12]

In spite of the imperfections of human nature and the continuing struggle to remain true to its principles in a changing
world, the Scott Bader Commonwealth represents an inspiring
success story. Fifty years after its foundation, the seeds planted
by Ernest Bader in 1951 have germinated far beyond the
confines of his own enterprise. Most notably, the Industrial
Common Ownership Movement (ICOM) developed out of an
initiative instigated largely by Scott Bader. During the 1960s
a small group of producers' co-ops, of which Scott Bader
was one, established an organization called the Society for
Democratic Integration in Industry. It changed its name to the
Industrial Common Ownership Movement in 1971.

ICOM was instrumental in the creation of the Industrial
Common Ownership Act in 1976, which began life as a private
member's bill won by David Watkins, MP for Consett, and
supported by an all-party group of MPs. This Act, combined
with the continuing work of ICOM and other bodies, has
played an important role in the resurgence of the co-operative
movement. In 1976 only one new enterprise was registered
with ICOM sponsorship. In 1977 this rose to 27 new enterprises, in 1978 there were 73, in 1979 there were 134, and
in 1980 there were 224. A small but significant co-operative
revolution had begun.

Today co-operatives are to be found in every sector of the
economy: from coal to construction, and from computers to
caring and catering. They are locally owned, creating and
retaining wealth and jobs in their communities. They are
democratically controlled, making democracy effective in the

workplace. They are free from the absentee control of remote shareholders who seek nothing from the companies in which they invest except short-term gain.

Co-operative enterprises remain small compared with the corporate giants of industry but they can still vary in size from a mere handful of members to a workforce of many hundreds. The multifarious types and size of co-operative enterprises can be gauged by looking at a representative cross-section. Delta T Services is a twenty-eight-person co-operative based in Cambridge which manufactures scientific instruments for environmental and industrial research. Started twenty-five years ago, it is at the cutting edge of technology. The Wrekin Care co-operative in Shropshire employs seventy-seven carers who provide home and day care to some three hundred dependent people. The Headstart Pre-School Centre is a co-operative nursery with a staff of twenty-nine who provide care for over seventy children on two sites in Preston.

Co-operatives such as Suma, based in Halifax, the Essential Trading Co-operative in Bristol, Green City Wholefoods in Glasgow, and Highland Wholefoods in Inverness have been in the vanguard of the wholesale supply of organic and wholefood products. They have a combined turnover of nearly £20 million. Poptel, the trade name of Soft Solution, provides Internet and online services from its three sites in London, Manchester and Yorkshire. Tower Colliery is a mine producing anthracite in the South Wales coalfield. Formerly part of British Coal, the pit reopened under democratic employee control in January 1995, employing 270 workers. Since then, production at the colliery has increased by 33 per cent to 540,000 tonnes. At the end of 1996 the co-operative announced pre-tax profits of £4 million.

This handful of examples, coupled with the continuing success of the Scott Bader Commonwealth, makes it clear that it is possible to both co-operate and prosper. Other examples of co-operative initiatives – both national and international – are discussed in the next chapter.

1 Papal Encyclica, *Rerum Novarum*, 1891.
2 Christopher Derrick, interview with Joseph Pearce, Wallington, Surrey, September 1996.
3 Solzhenitsyn, *Rebuilding Russia*, p. 33.
4 Ibid., p. 30.
5 Ibid., p. 31.
6 Ibid., p. 32.
7 Ibid., p. 34.
8 Schumacher, *Small Is Beautiful*, p. 230.
9 Ibid., p. 231.
10 Ibid., pp. 236–7.
11 Discussion with Joseph Pearce at Scott Bader Commonwealth, Wollaston, Northamptonshire, 9 November 1999.
12 Ibid.

17

The Proof of the Pudding

I am one of those who believe that the cure for centralization is decentralization. It has been described as a paradox. There is apparently something elvish and fantastic about saying that when capital has come to be too much in the hands of the few, the right thing is to restore it into the hands of the many.[1]

G.K. Chesterton

No appraisal of the role of co-operatives in Britain would be complete without paying due attention to what can be regarded as the grandfather of the co-operative movement in Britain, Equity Shoes of Leicester. It has been trading for well over a century.

Equity Shoes was born out of the labour pains of industrial strife. In 1886 the workers in a Leicester shoe factory approached the management to ask for a fair share of the profits which their labour had produced, arguing that profit-sharing would create an incentive for them to work even harder for the company. The management did not agree and the disgruntled employees went on strike in protest. The strikers read an account of a stove factory in France which was run on co-operative lines and were inspired to attempt a similar scheme in Leicester. A meeting was called on 16 September 1886 and the Leicester Co-operative Boot and Shoe Manufacturing Society Ltd, later to change its name to Equity Shoes, was born.

In the spring of 1887 twenty-one determined pioneers started to produce shoes. From the very beginning the co-op established a reputation for quality. The *Boot and Shoe Trade Journal* reported in 1888 that the shoes produced by the co-op 'show an amount of care and finish not often surpassed … The quality of the tops leaves nothing to be desired, and the bottoming reflects the greatest credit upon the workmen who finished them for they have expended upon them an amount of artistic skill, combined with quality of workmanship, deserving of the highest praise.'[2]

A century later, with annual turnover in excess of £4 million, Equity's president, S.W. Pepper, could afford to speak with pride about the co-op's history and with confidence about its future:

> Not in their wildest dreams could those brave men in 1886 have thought the Society would celebrate its Centenary. From such tiny beginnings the 'Committee' could never have thought that 'their Society' could become so hugely successful and so significant in the world of shoe manufacturing … For the sake of those of the past and their social experiment, and of those of the future who inherit so much, I hope Equity will continue its success through to its bicentenary …[3]

In an industry which has been devastated by the impact of low-cost imports, Equity Shoes is one of relatively few survivors. This is itself a powerful indication that co-ops are able to compete with the best of the rest of industry. Furthermore, while many of its domestic competitors continue to struggle, Equity has started its second century as it commenced its first – with a reputation for high-quality products. It has a niche in the market, specializing in quality fashion shoes, boots and sandals for women in the thirty-five-plus age group. Every week the co-op receives about two dozen letters from satisfied customers. In March 1990 a report in the *Leicester Mercury* disclosed that Equity had 'considerably lifted turnover and doubled its customer base in the past ten years'.[4] It now employs more than two hundred people and has a thriving export market. 'Quality is the key note,' says Doug Steel, Equity's general manager. 'We cannot hope to compete on price with countries such as Portugal, which use cheap labour, but we can compete on quality.' He added that the co-op was 'quietly confident' about the future.[5]

This cursory glance at the rise of the co-operative movement in Britain should not obscure the role played by co-operatives internationally. In many countries the co-operative role in industry is much more prominent and successful than it is in the United Kingdom. The Mondragon group of producers' co-ops mentioned in chapter 16, employing some eighteen thousand people in the Spanish Basque country, is perhaps the best-known co-operative success story. The Mondragon 'experiment', started in the 1950s by a Basque priest, Father Arizmendiarrieta, has been much written about, has been the subject of television documentaries, and is generally held as the model to be emulated worldwide.

Mondragon is, however, by no means the only example which could be followed. In Italy producers' co-ops have been equally successful and employ about half a million people. The Italian movement has continued to grow rapidly during the 1990s, both through the establishment of new firms and through worker takeovers of existing firms. Most successful are the building co-ops, some of which are very large, employing, in the case of the largest, as many as three thousand people.

Grassroots Reality

Nonetheless, the larger picture should never distract attention from the grassroots reality of human-scale economics. Most co-operatives are small in size and, alongside the small business sector, should form the basis of a small and beautiful economy. More can be learned about the reality of working in a co-operative from the experience of a handful of people in one tiny co-op than from any amount of abstract global theorizing. The personal testimonies of those working in one such co-op, the Treehouse restaurant in Norwich, form a fitting conclusion to this discussion on the need to co-operate.

Jane Taylor, a founding member of the Treehouse, explains that its roots 'go back to the early eighties when a small group of people including myself and Annie Whiteman took over the running of the café at Premises, as the Arts Centre was known in those days'. The co-op was formed in 1983 when the restaurant's success necessitated that it be placed on a proper business footing. 'By this time a group of seven or eight of us had become involved in running the café, all committed to the idea of a wholefood, vegetarian restaurant. We all got along well, although there were moments of high drama in the kitchen! Nobody wanted to take on sole responsibility for the business and anyway we believed that everybody involved, from cook to washer-up, had an equal part to play in the running of the restaurant, so forming a co-op was the obvious thing to do.' The co-op was formed with assistance from the

Norwich Co-operative Development Agency.

The early days were a real struggle, as Jane Taylor recalls:

When we took over the café we inherited a very basic kitchen that was probably an environmental health nightmare and we worked hard for little wages to get the café established. We were very lucky that because of an informal arrangement with Premises we didn't pay rent. So we didn't have to come up with a business plan or get a big loan to start things going. We were just a group of people interested in food who wanted to work in a place with like-minded people.

The success of the café took everyone by surprise, giving those involved the confidence to move to Dove Street, where the restaurant above the Rainbow wholefood shop had become empty. Unable to call themselves 'The Café at Premises' any longer, someone, in a moment of inspiration, came up with 'the Treehouse' as an appropriate name. 'Financially the first few months in Dove Street were a real struggle,' remembers Taylor. 'It's amazing what you can do with a few carrots and turnips and a handful of beans! We survived and the restaurant continues.'

In the years that followed, the Treehouse built a reputation as one of the finest restaurants in Norwich. Even committed carnivores were grudgingly converted to the variety of imaginative recipes on the restaurant's meat-free menu. In December 1994 the co-op achieved national recognition when it was named as Restaurant of the Month in *BBC Vegetarian Good Food* magazine. Today, more than fifteen years after its formation, it continues to prosper. Turnover has increased every year and in 1998 reached £160,000.

The co-op still has only eight members, though the personnel have changed over the years. Apart from sharing a commitment to vegetarianism and co-operative ownership, its members have come from all walks of life. Teachers, office workers, graduates and a cleaner from the local theatre have all graced the ranks. One former member was an electrical engineer on nuclear submarines before he joined the Treehouse.

New members are not required to make any financial input on joining and are free to leave after a month's notice. According to the current members, those who join are attracted to the different mode of employment offered by the co-op and they insist that nobody has left disillusioned with the principle of common ownership. The work is physically demanding but deeply satisfying. The members are self-motivating and are paid daily. They occasionally award themselves profit shares.

'I have worked at the Treehouse restaurant for nearly three years,' says Darren Slowther, 'the longest period I have ever spent working full time for the same company. I've had many other jobs … but all had the same thing in common: a complete lack of job satisfaction.' He attributes the job satisfaction he has found at the Treehouse 'to the way the business is run and the relationship I have with the other co-op members'.

Since joining the co-op, he says that 'work has become more a part of life rather than a detached chore, because we all know who we are working with and for – ourselves. There is an intimacy involved in working for a co-op that is missing in larger organizations. Additionally, there is far more to the job than actual kitchen work and it is this variation and responsibility that also adds to the job. Day-to-day contact with customers also provides immediate feedback on the quality of your work, which can give greater encouragement.'

A similar sense of the satisfaction that comes from sharing responsibility was expressed by fellow member Clare Bufton:

I get so much out of working as part of the co-op. All of us are equally responsible for the business and this makes the job very fulfilling. It also means that it is important, yet easy, to be very self-motivated. We all share the everyday tasks, which makes working as part of a team easier, as we all appreciate the difficulties and stresses of the job. A huge achievement for me is that I've really developed my confidence and assertiveness since joining my lovely workmates – this is a result of being on an equal level with them.

Joel Rodker is a relatively new member of the co-op who joined in the summer of 1999. Yet his commitment is as thorough as that of his colleagues. He speaks of its 'lively and friendly atmosphere', adding that it 'provides a feeling of homeliness and comfort in the heart of the city'. It is important, he insists, 'that the restaurant has its roots in the local community … In addition, the Treehouse provides an example of how a success-ful local business can be run co-operatively, without the need for a boss-led hierarchy and without the need to compromise on a range of environmental and business principles.'

Ian Carey compares the contentment he has found at the Treehouse with the alienation he experienced in his previous working life. Spending eight years on the shop floor as a panel beater, he was promoted to work in reception and started deal-ing with the public. He ended up as assistant customer service manager for Eagle Star but found himself increasingly dissatis-fied. 'At Eagle Star I became more and more disillusioned with big company ethics. I felt more like a number than a person, my identity taken away and a big corporate badge put in its place.' In contrast, the Treehouse enabled him to feel part of a team, 'no, a family'. 'It allows consistent self-improvement as you are involved in all aspects of running the business, from cleaning to cooking to decision making. The Treehouse allows you to be yourself. It's hard work, but we have lots of fun.'

Tonia Mihill was working as a secondary school teacher in London when she applied to join the Treehouse in 1994. 'I had tried quite a variety of other jobs,' she says, 'and had ended up feeling bored, frustrated or exploited and sometimes all three! When I applied to join the co-op, I was attracted to being part of a business which has an ethical basis and to the idea of working co-operatively. I have not been disappointed. This is the first job that I can say I have consistently enjoyed.' She has a healthy sense of humour, finding amusement in the fact that involvement in every aspect of the business means everything 'from the financial planning to cleaning the toilets … If you see us scrubbing our surfaces, we could be contemplating our cash flows!'

'No Freedom Without Discipline'

There is, however, a serious side. Rigid rules and routines are 'absolutely necessary', she insists, 'particularly when there is no one giving orders. There is no freedom without discipline.' That last statement illustrates that Mihill has a philosophical approach to life which both underpins and transcends her whole character. This is evident in all that she says about the Treehouse:

> One of the constraints that we work within is trying to cater for a variety of special diets – dairy-free, sugar-free, gluten-free and fermentation-free being the most common. We also aim to have a menu which is varied and interesting. The freedom and creativity arise from the fact that within these constraints and others such as budget, time and facilities, we can cook whatever we like. It's like jazz or blues, the structure is the beginning not

219

the end and somehow makes it easier to improve new combinations – and for those occasions when inspiration is exhausted, we all have some standard numbers to fall back on!

There is also clearly freedom in the fact that we can change our routines, improve our working practices, introduce new products very easily. We have meetings fortnightly to discuss all aspects of running the business and once a decision is made, it can be implemented immediately. In a small co-operative, everyone really does make a difference.

There are other ways that being a co-operative is different from much of the mainstream business world. For a start, we are not simply concerned to maximize profits at the expense of our own or anyone else's health or well-being. We aim to give each other the flexibility to meet the demands of our lives outside work and to pursue other activities. Whenever possible we buy fairly traded products and organic produce and we wish to provide good-quality food at affordable prices ... As members of the co-op, we have to learn how to value each other's unique contributions rather than dwelling on perceived shortcomings and how to negotiate, compromise and resolve conflict in order to enable our differences to be strengths...

The Treehouse is not an ideal, it is real. We do not have a preset script which requires us to wish you a nice day, ask if you enjoyed your meal or smile a prescribed number of times (we don't even think the customer is always right!). We do not always get on, we struggle and argue but we also support and forgive each other, laugh a lot and cook great food almost all of the time and absolutely amazing food for some of the time! We care about what we do and the way in which we conduct ourselves as a business in our community and the wider world. The Treehouse is real and honest in a world too concerned with artificial and seductive, but misleading, images.

Tonia Mihill has put the case for co-operatives in a sublimely beautiful nutshell. She and the other members of the Treehouse have shown that the proof of the pudding is indeed in the eating. When the people who produce the pudding are as happy as those who consume it we are surely approaching not only the real, but the ideal.

1 Chesterton, *The Outline of Sanity*, p. 4.
2 S.W. Pepper, *A History of Equity Shoes Limited*, Leicester: Equity Shoes Ltd, 1986.
3 Ibid.
4 *Leicester Mercury*, 9 March 1990.
5 Ibid.

18

Ends and Beginnings

Science and engineering produce 'know-how'; but 'know-how' is nothing by itself; it is a means without an end, a mere potentiality, an unfinished sentence. 'Know-how' is no more a culture than a piano is music.[1]

E.F. Schumacher

The theme of *Small Is Beautiful* is that people matter. And if people matter, so do all other forms of life. Humanity is part of an integrated and ordered living creation and cannot exist in isolation from the biosphere that sustains it. If we destroy life on our planet we are ultimately destroying ourselves. Biocide is suicide.

For whatever reason, humanity holds the role of steward. Since the dawn of history, human beings have manipulated their physical surroundings to their own advantage. We continue to do so, except that we now have, through modern technology, powers that were not available to previous generations. It is clear that we do not know how to use these powers properly. Science has given humanity knowledge but not the wisdom to use that knowledge prudently. Techno-man, devoid of any metaphysical understanding, knows *how* to do things without knowing *why* or *whether* they should be done. We do them because we can, not because we should. Indeed, we do many things we shouldn't merely because we can.

Schumacher insisted that humanity needed the transmission of ideas of *value*, first and foremost, and that the need to transmit know-how must take second place. It is, he wrote, 'obviously somewhat foolhardy to put great powers into the hands of people without making sure that they have a reasonable idea of what to do with them. At present, there can be little doubt that the whole of mankind is in mortal danger, not because we are short of scientific and technological know-how, but because we tend to use it destructively, without wisdom.'[2]

The potential tragedy of the situation is that this increased power to influence life on earth, for better or worse, has arrived at a time when humanity has turned its back on the wisdom to be found in the study of philosophy. The meaning of life is not, it seems, important to our education. Instead the modern world has sacrificed concepts of right and wrong, of ethics and morals, on the altars of technolatry and economic growth. While science takes centre stage, philosophy is not to be found anywhere on the national curriculum. Children are not expected to ask why, merely to know how. Why is this? Why has humanity turned its back on traditional philosophy? Why has it rejected the wisdom of the ages? Why does it look instead towards technological innovations and instant gratifications, towards the new and the now?

Living Tradition

Schumacher discusses this question at length in *Small Is Beautiful*. All traditional philosophy is, he wrote, 'an attempt to create an orderly system of ideas by which to live and to interpret the world'.[3] According to Professor Kuhn, whom Schumacher quoted with approval, the ancient Greeks conceived philosophy as 'one single effort of the human mind to interpret the system of signs and so to relate man to the world as a comprehensive order within which a place is assigned to him'. The philosophy of the Greeks, particularly that espoused by Plato and Aristotle, was adopted and Christianized, or 'Christened', by later philosophers such as St Augustine and St Thomas Aquinas. There is, therefore, a living tradition of western philosophy stretching back for almost two and a half thousand years. Schumacher had made a study of this synthesis of Christian and classical thought and he compared it with the emptiness with which the modern world had replaced it:

> *The classical-Christian culture of the late Middle Ages supplied man with a very complete and astonishingly coherent interpretation of signs, i.e. a system of vital ideas giving a most detailed picture of man, the universe, and man's place in the universe. This system, however, has been shattered and fragmented, and the result is bewilderment and estrangement...*[4]

By the twentieth century, many shared Bertrand Russell's atheistic assumption that the whole universe is simply 'the outcome of accidental collocations of atoms' and his conclusion from this that 'only on the firm foundation of unyielding despair can the soul's habitation henceforth be safely built'. Similarly, Sir Fred Hoyle, the celebrated astronomer, epitomized the modernist angst when he spoke of 'the truly dreadful situation in which we find ourselves. Here we are in this wholly fantastic universe with scarcely a clue as to whether our existence has any real significance.'[5] Schumacher believed that this estrangement, or alienation, this 'encounter with nothingness', 'breeds loneliness and despair ... cynicism, empty gestures of defiance, as we can see in the greater part of existentialist philosophy and general literature today ... So, what is the cause of estrangement? Never has science been more triumphant; never has man's power over his environment been more complete or his progress faster. It cannot be a lack of know-how that causes the despair...'[6]

The Insufficiency of Science

Since science can only provide know-how, not wisdom, it cannot produce ideas or values by which we can live. It cannot find the cause of the feeling of estrangement, the feeling that life is empty, meaningless, devoid of purpose. It can only show us how things work, not why things are.

If, however, science is purely factual, then scientism is pure folly because it attempts to draw philosophical conclusions from scientific premises. Since the 'how' of science and the 'why' of philosophy are essentially different, it is nonsense to suggest that philosophical truth can be derived from scientific fact. It is an attempt to quantify the qualitative. It is like trying to measure the beauty of a sunset by examining it under a microscope. Science can define a sunset within its own strict physical limitations. It can explain how light passing through the atmosphere when the sun is at a certain angle makes the particles in the atmosphere appear various shades of red and gold. In other words, it can explain how the sunset works. It cannot explain why the sunset is beautiful.

Similarly, science cannot explain the existence of metaphysical realities that are part of everybody's personality or psyche. Take, for example, the existence of faith. Even atheists have faith

– they can't help having it. Bertrand Russell's belief that the universe is only an accidental collocation of atoms is a statement of faith. He cannot prove that all the atoms are there by accident. He can only believe it through an act of faith. It is one of life's many paradoxes that it requires a leap of faith to believe in anything, and it is perhaps evidence of a divine sense of humour that it also requires a leap of faith to believe in nothing.

Muddled Thinking

In *Small Is Beautiful*, Schumacher singled out a number of leading ideas which were the product of this muddled thinking. Darwin's theory of evolution, for example, may be a scientifically correct, i.e. a factually accurate, description of how the species of life have developed. Yet it has given rise to various forms of 'Darwinism' which seek to make all reality, physical and metaphysical, conform with this particular theory of biological development.

Social Darwinists believe that because biological life has 'evolved' as part of a natural and automatic process into higher forms from primitive beginnings, society as a whole must be always 'evolving' or 'progressing'. Social Darwinism insists that such human progress is unstoppable. This belief in inexorable progress has fuelled the dangerous assumption that any problems caused to the well-being of humanity or to the planet's ecosystem by the 'onward march' of technology will always be overcome. Social Darwinism leads to the Micawber Factor we mentioned before, the belief that 'something will turn up'. It breeds complacency in those it afflicts, spreading apathy and inertia in the face of the crisis facing the modern world. This 'progressive' theory is actually an enemy of genuine progress.

Another erroneous by-product of Darwin's theory is the idea that natural selection is applicable to every aspect of life. This particular aberration, or mutation, of the theory of evolution has found expression in what may be termed economic Darwinism. According to this theory, competition, natural selection and the survival of the fittest are the dominant forces at work in individuals and, therefore, in the economy also. Since these forces are embedded in our genes they are unstoppable. We are, whether we like it or not, essentially selfish. Consequently, since we can't help acting selfishly we may as well make a virtue of necessity. Economic Darwinism is the enshrinement of selfishness.

Linked to economic Darwinism is the more general belief in economic determinism. This view maintains that all the higher manifestations of human life, such as religion, philosophy and the arts, are only the by-products of the material life process. They are what Marx called 'the phantasmagorias in the brains of men', little more than superficial constructs that only disguise and promote underlying economic interests. They are a diversion from the real driving force of human history, which is economics. According to economic determinists the whole of history is an economic struggle. Economics determines everything.

On this level there is a remarkable similarity between capitalism and communism. Both systems work on the assumption that economics is the dominant factor in human life. For the Marxist, religion is the opiate of the people. For the capitalist it is, like everything else, merely a matter of consumer choice. Both are united in the tacit belief that religious truth is subject to the economic facts of life. Again, since economic determinism places self-interest at the centre of life, it is selfish in its very essence.

Sigmund Freud countered the supposition that all life is driven by avarice by declaring that it is in fact driven by lust.

Freud and his followers believed that all the higher manifestations of life could be explained, or explained away, by reducing them to 'the dark stirrings of a subconscious mind' influenced by 'unfulfilled incest-wishes during childhood and early adolescence'.[7] In practical terms, the belief that life is dominated by lust has the same result as the belief that it is dominated by greed. Both systems maintain that the desire for self-gratification is the ultimate purpose of life.

Selfishness Enshrined

Embracing these various attempts to enshrine selfishness is the general idea of relativism, which denies the existence of all absolutes. Relativists deny the existence of objective reality and all meaningful notions of truth. Since Truth does not exist, or at any rate is unknowable, my 'truth' is as valid as yours. Truth is in the eye of the beholder. It is only an opinion, a product of the individual's imagination. This is the ultimate selfishness. It places the Self at the centre of reality, at the centre of the universe.

These various ideas that have gained such influence in the modern world may have flowered in the nineteenth century but they had their collective roots in the late Renaissance and in the so-called Enlightenment. It was at this time that people began to reject traditional western philosophy, with its quest for objective understanding and wisdom, in favour of an egocentric view of reality. Prior to the Enlightenment, philosophers believed that man was part of an objectively ascertainable universe. The best way of understanding man was to understand Creation and man's part in it. Following the Enlightenment, people began to insist that the best way of understanding man was man, regardless of his environment. This man-centred view of reality set in motion a reductionist train of thought.

Placing man at the centre meant that the self was placed at the centre. Placing the self at the centre eventually led to a denial of any truth beyond the self. From a denial of any truth beyond the self it was a short step to the denial of truth itself, and indeed to a denial of any meaningful self. In pursuing himself without regard to others, man had disappeared into the murky recesses of his own mind.

The other dominant modern idea which Schumacher singled out for particular attention is positivism. This in many ways is a reaction to relativism, though it makes the same fundamental errors. Positivism holds that valid knowledge is attainable only through the methods employed by the natural sciences. No knowledge can be regarded as genuine unless it is based on observable phenomena. Positivism, wrote Schumacher, 'is solely interested in "know-how" and denies the possibility of objective knowledge about meaning and purpose of any kind'.[8] The logical absurdity of the positivist position, and that of its relativist relation, was highlighted by Schumacher in incisive terms: 'Relativism and positivism, of course, are purely metaphysical doctrines with the peculiar and ironical distinction that they deny the validity of all metaphysics, including themselves.'[9]

Why, one could be tempted to ask, should we concern ourselves with 'obscure' questions of philosophy when our world is in imminent danger? Why bother with nebulous metaphysics when what is needed is practical action and physical solutions to the world's problems? The answer is simple. There can be no solution to the world's problems until their causes are properly understood. The problems have been caused by a humanity that is in thrall to a view of itself and its environment which is essentially self-centred. If selfishness is a virtue, the ultimate reality, is it any wonder that the world has no other goal than unbridled economic growth so that the feeding frenzy of consumerism can be kept going? Similarly, if we are driven by greed or lust, whether we like it or not, there is no point in fighting it. Self-control, self-sacrifice and self-limitation are a waste of time. They are unnatural because they go against the grain of our predetermined instincts. Why not go with the flow and seek self-gratification as the only purpose of life?

Questions and Answers

Clearly we have to ask fundamental questions about our own nature before we can find the answers needed to counter the egocentric philosophies. Who are we? Why are we? Do we have a higher nature that can rise above greed or lust? Do we have a higher purpose than self-gratification? Only by answering these questions, and persuading others to accept our answers, can we hope to change people's attitudes and consequently their actions.

'We have become confused as to what our convictions really are,' wrote Schumacher. 'The great ideas of the nineteenth century may fill our minds in one way or another, but our hearts do not believe in them all the same. Mind and heart are at war with one another, not, as is commonly asserted, reason and faith. Our reason has become beclouded by an extraordinary, blind and unreasonable faith in a set of fantastic and life-destroying ideas inherited from the nineteenth century. It is the foremost task of our reason to recover a truer faith than that.'[10]

In the final analysis we cannot even begin to solve the problems facing humanity and the world it inhabits until we understand ourselves and our purpose, the end for which we exist. This will require hard work and courageous thinking. Schumacher, characteristically, ends *Small Is Beautiful* on a practical note, showing us where to direct our efforts:

Everywhere people ask: 'What can I actually do?' The answer is as simple as it is disconcerting: we can, each of us, work to put our own inner house in order. The guidance we need for this work cannot be found in science or technology, the value of which utterly depends on the ends they serve; but it can still be found in the traditional wisdom of mankind.[11]

1 Schumacher, *Small Is Beautiful*, p. 66.
2 Ibid.
3 Ibid., p. 69.
4 Ibid.
5 Ibid., pp. 69–70.
6 Ibid., p. 70.
7 Ibid., p. 72.
8 Ibid.
9 Ibid., p. 73.
10 Ibid., p. 76.
11 Ibid., pp. 249–50.

19

Begin Here

Somehow we have got to find the integrating principle for our lives, the creative power that sustains our balance in motion, and we have got to do it quickly … The task is urgent; we must not push it into the future; we must not leave it to others: we must do it ourselves, and we must begin now and here.[1]

Dorothy L. Sayers

'The guidance we need … can still be found in the traditional wisdom of mankind.' The words with which Schumacher concluded *Small Is Beautiful* are a clarion cry to a beleaguered humanity, a call to action. What then is 'traditional wisdom' and why has it been neglected by the modern world?

In 1976, the year before he died, Schumacher endeavoured to answer this question in an article in *Resurgence* magazine:

The fundamental question, asked by all peoples at all times, is 'What is man?' And the answer given by the universal tradition of mankind is that man is a compound of spirit, soul, and body…

The modern West is the only significant exception. All other civilizations are – or at any rate used to be – primarily interested in spiritual matters; they saw the spirit as the divine and, generally, immortal element, equipped with a psychosomatic instrument, the embodied soul or, if you like, the ensouled body.

Naturally, if there is such an element which is divine and immortal, it deserves infinitely more attention than its instrument, the soul-body, which is so dependent, so changeable, and so obviously mortal. Hence the whole of life revolved around the spirit as the only 'reality'…

In Europe, we have moved away from all this during the last three centuries or so. The modern West is not preoccupied with spiritual matters, but with material matters instead.[2]

The historical process by which the West rejected the spiritual in favour of the material was discussed in the previous chapter. Today, with 'western values' being exported to every corner of the world through the increasing encroachment of the multinationals and the spread of consumerism, the battle lines are being drawn between the spiritual and the material across the globe. The triumph of the West means the stifling of the human spirit and, as we have seen, the destruction of the environment.

Chronological Snobbery

The battle between spiritual values and materialism is a battle of conflicting ideas. On one side is traditional wisdom and on the other is intellectual fashion. In reality, however, the two conflicting views rarely engage in stimulating contest. Instead traditional wisdom is simply held in scorn by its fashionable enemy. In a dismissive display of chronological snobbery, the modern materialist sees the struggle as one between the latest knowledge and ancient, i.e. ignorant and old-fashioned, error. For the 'modern', or 'postmodern', it is simply a struggle between progress and reaction, between the advanced and the backward, the enlightened and the ignorant. Since everything – biology, society, humanity, history – is 'progressing', each new generation is seen, implicitly and subconsciously at least, as inherently superior to preceding generations. Things can only get better … Taken to a fanciful extreme, one can imagine these chronological snobs deriding Plato and Aristotle, should the philosophers be miraculously transported to the modern world, because, as ignorant 'peasants', they could not drive a car or surf the net.

In the essay quoted above, Schumacher cited Eugene Black, a former president of the World Bank, as a classic example of the chronological snobbery which is intent on trampling tradition into the dirt of history so that material 'progress' can emerge triumphant. In his lecture on 'The Age of Economic Development', Black exhibited the patronizing arrogance with which the organization he once headed treats the traditions of the world: 'We are talking about transforming whole societies and creating new traditions to replace traditions which have been rendered tragically inadequate by the passing of time.' It is pointless trying to argue with this assessment because Eugene Black refuses to accept the validity of any conflicting ideas or ideologies. In fact, ideas and ideologies are themselves a barrier to progress. 'There is,' he said, 'real hope that people will take ideology less seriously simply because they will be too busy … it is largely … by not taking ideology too seriously that the western world today enjoys democracy and freedom as well as the highest material living standards'.

One of the freedoms offered by Eugene Black's economic religion is liberation from all morality. It was, he said, necessary to 'render the language of economics ... morally antiseptic'. The gospel according to Eugene Black appears to amount to nothing but the maxim 'Get Rich, – Be Happy'. And yet even this may be too complex. Some smart Alec might start asking awkward questions, based on some dreaded ideology, about what exactly constitutes happiness. Perhaps the gospel should be simplified still further, to 'Get Rich'; or as Black put it: 'We try to remove the taint of ideology from the language of economics and thus relate that language solely to the end of promoting higher material living standards.' Thus, in an absurd paradox, humanity has climbed the centuries-old ladder of progress to reach at last the lowest common denominator.

Eugene Black's simplistic gospel was given a more eloquent spin by Professor Donald J. Dewey, of Duke University in the United States:

> The concern for efficiency and progress is – and always has been – secular in that it condemns all religious restraints that are inimical to higher man-hour productivity. This concern is unromantic in that it will not sacrifice national income in order to maintain a happy peasantry or a culture-carrying leisure class. It is materialistic in that happiness is regarded as a more pressing goal – if not a more worthy goal – than salvation. And above all, it is optimistic in that it supposes that the sum of human happiness is increased by growing wealth.[3]

Fashionable Hedonism

Such a view may be intellectually fashionable but it is anything but new. It is merely the old doctrine of hedonism dressed up in the fashionable clothes of economic determinism. Hedonism, the doctrine that sees the pursuit of maximum pleasure as the mainspring of human action, was first put forward by Aristippus of Cyrene four centuries before the birth of Christ. Unlike Professor Dewey, however, the ancients realized that hedonism raised two fundamental problems. First, it was necessary to devise some method of weighing pleasures against pains, a '*felicific calculus*'; second, it was necessary to differentiate between intense transient pleasures and moderate but enduring ones. Unfortunately, modern hedonists champion the creed, believing it somehow to be new, without understanding the problems.

This is all very well – or not – in theory but how does it measure up in practice? The impact of such a philosophy, for that is what it is regardless of Eugene Black's protestations to the contrary, has been devastating. Modern hedonists, armed with technology and intent only on pleasing themselves, have destroyed the living environment both physically and metaphysically. Physically, they are destroying the ecological balance that sustains the health and life-sustaining power of the biosphere upon which they ultimately depend. Metaphysically, they are destroying the natural *beauty* of life through the physical and social damage caused by unbridled selfishness. This issue was discussed by Schumacher in an essay entitled 'Message from the Universe':

> ...it is not the great numbers of the world's poor that are endangering Spaceship Earth but the relatively small numbers of the world's rich. The threat to the environment, and in particular to world resources and the biosphere, comes from the life-style of the rich societies and not from that of the poor. Even in the poor societies there are some rich people, and as long as they adhere to their traditional culture they do very little, if any, harm. It is only when they become 'westernized' that

damage to the environment ensues ... It is not simply a matter
of rich or poor ... It is a matter of life-styles. A poor American
may do much more ecological damage than a rich Asian.[4]

Hedonism Versus Self-limitation

Since our lifestyles spring from our most fundamental attitudes
and convictions it is, whether we like it or not, a question of
metaphysics or religion. The choice is between the hedonism
of materialism and the self-limitation practised by the advocates of traditional wisdom. The cultures of the East, and those
of the West prior to the rise of materialism, are the products
of a sustained spiritual struggle, conducted over thousands of
years, 'to uphold and develop what is good in human beings
and to weaken and control what is evil; to promote in every way
the Good, the True and the Beautiful, as Plato would say; but,
above all to obtain salvation by the way of Knowledge'.[5]

This knowledge is not the sort offered by science and
technology, which, being merely factual, is only useful on a
material level. It is a metaphysical knowledge that leads to
deeper understanding and wisdom. It is the 'knowledge that
sets you free', offering greater insight into ourselves, others,
the source of Truth and our higher purpose within it. It is the
pursuit of the highest common factors of life, not its lowest
common denominators.

The essential unity of the traditional wisdom of East and
West was discussed by Ananda Coomaraswamy, leader of the
twentieth-century cultural revival in India:

If we leave out ... the 'modernistic' and individual philosophies
of today, and consider only the great tradition of the magnani-
mous philosophers, whose philosophy was a religion that had to

> *be lived if it was to be understood, it will soon be found that*
> *the distinctions of culture in East and West, or for that matter*
> *North and South, are comparable only to those of dialects; all*
> *are speaking what is essentially one and the same spiritual*
> *language, employing different words, but expressing the same*
> *ideas, and very often by means of identical idioms. Otherwise*
> *stated, there is a universally intelligible language, not only*
> *verbal but also visual, of the fundamental ideas on which the*
> *different civilizations have been founded.*[6]

This intrinsic wisdom has a different approach to economic questions from that espoused by modern materialists. The materialist insists on the anti-traditional and anti-spiritual approach, believing that all religions are reactionary and that the self-limitation endemic in the major spiritual traditions is an obstacle to economic growth. Meanwhile those who adhere to tradition insist that meaningful and sustainable economic development is impossible without the strength and purity of spiritual truth. The contrast between the two contending philosophies was summed up succinctly by Schumacher: 'The one is modern and Western; the other is derived from indigenous traditions of great antiquity. The one puts the accent on quantity; the other, on quality. The one is mainly concerned with the satisfactions derivable from consumption; the other, with the dignity and creativity of people as producers. The one degrades labour and then tries to save it; the other ennobles labour and uses it freely.'[7]

It was, said Schumacher, a straightforward choice between serving either God or Mammon. 'It is a part of the modern error to believe that this is equivalent to a choice between poverty and riches. It is not. On the contrary, all appearances notwithstanding, the service of Mammon is not rewarded by lasting prosperity, but by cataclysmic disaster. It is the service of God – or of Truth, as Asia would say – that alone leads to lasting well-being on this earth.'[8]

A Realistic Order of Priorities

The cataclysmic disaster looming before us is the accelerating breakdown of the earth's biosphere as mother earth buckles under the strain of the cancerous greed which is spreading throughout the world. As Schumacher observed, the challenge to materialism is no longer coming solely from the saints and sages who have warned against it down the ages, but from the environment which sustains all life on earth. 'At all times, in all societies, the saints and sages have warned against materialism and pleaded for a more realistic order of priorities. The languages have differed, the symbols have varied, but the essential message has always been the same – in modern terms: Get your priorities right; in Christian terms: "Seek ye first the kingdom of God, and all these things (the material things which you also need) shall be added unto you".'[9]

Today this perennial message is being echoed by our natural environment. It is almost as though the very stones of the earth were crying out for a return to a proper balance in humanity's relationship with Life. Our continuing failure to heed the warnings of sages, saints, the prophets and the planet itself, can only have disastrous consequences. Schumacher again:

> Everything points to the fact that what is most needed today is a revision of the ends which all our efforts are meant to serve. And this implies that above all else we need the development of a life-style which accords the material things their proper, legitimate place, which is secondary and not primary. The chance

239

of mitigating the rate of resource depletion or of bringing harmony into the relationship between people and their environment is non-existent as long as there is no idea anywhere of a life-style which treats Enough as good and More-than-enough as being of evil. Here lies the real challenge, and no amount of technical ingenuity can evade it. The environment, in its own language, is telling us that we are moving along the wrong path, and acceleration in the wrong direction will not put us right. When people call for 'moral choices' in accordance with 'new values', this means nothing unless it means the over-coming of the materialistic life-style of the modern world and the reinstatement of some authentic moral teaching.[10]

Schumacher alluded to the folly, not to say the arrogance, of the presumption that the modern world, which was 'more enslaved by material preoccupations than anyone before us', could discover any 'new' values that our ancestors had not discovered already. On the contrary, the 'authentic moral teaching' was nothing other than the perennial moral teaching of sacred tradition. The roots of the violence we do to ourselves, to our neighbours and to our environment had been discussed for centuries by moral philosophers. In the West, Christian philosophers taught that moral violence is sin and that the disharmony it causes is the bitter fruit of sin. The modern world denies the existence of sin in theory while indulging it with enthusiasm in practice. As a concept sin is out of fashion, as a recreation it is all the rage.

The relationship between sin and the problems confronting the modern world inspired Schumacher to take an interest in Dante, and through Dante he was introduced to the writing of Dorothy L. Sayers, describing her as 'one of the finest commentators on Dante as well as on modern society'.[11] In *A Guide for the Perplexed*, Schumacher quoted at length from Sayers's *Introductory Papers on Dante*, which had been published in 1954:

> *That the Inferno is a picture of human society in a state of sin and corruption, everybody will readily agree. And since we are today fairly well convinced that society is in a bad way and not necessarily evolving in the direction of perfectibility, we find it easy enough to recognize the various stages by which the deep of corruption is reached. Futility; lack of a living faith; the drift into loose morality, greedy consumption, financial irresponsibility, and uncontrolled bad temper; a self-opinionated and obstinate individualism; violence, sterility, and lack of reverence for life and property including one's own; the exploitation of sex, the debasing of language by advertisement and propaganda, the commercializing of religion, the pandering to superstition and the conditioning of people's minds by mass-hysteria and 'spellbinding' of all kinds, venality and string-pulling in public affairs, hypocrisy, dishonesty in material things, intellectual dishonesty, the fomenting of discord (class against class, nation against nation) for what one can get out of it, the falsification and destruction of all the means of communication; the exploitation of the lowest and stupidest mass-emotions; treachery even to the fundamentals of kinship, country, the chosen friend, and the sworn allegiance: these are the all-too-recognizable stages that lead to the cold death of society and the extinguishing of all civilized relations.*

'What an array of divergent problems!' Schumacher exclaimed after quoting this passage. 'Yet people go on clamouring for "solutions", and become angry when they are told that the restoration of society must come from within and cannot come from without.'[12]

Deadly Sins

In his essay 'The Roots of Violence', Schumacher again quotes extensively from Dorothy L. Sayers with regard to the Christian teaching of the Seven Deadly Sins, namely Lust, Wrath, Gluttony, Avarice, Envy, Sloth and Pride. The committing of these sins not only does violence to the soul of the individual but spreads that violence like a contagion through the society in which the individual lives. Thus, wrote Sayers, 'the sin of Gluttony, of Greed, of over-much stuffing of ourselves, is the sin that has delivered us over into the power of the machine … it is the great curse of Gluttony that it ends by destroying all sense of the precious, the unique, the irreplaceable.' The waste which is caused by 'sheer gluttonous consumption' produces 'all the slop and swill that pour down the sewers over which the palace of Gluttony is built'.[13]

Envy hates to see other men happy, wrote Sayers:

> The names by which it offers itself to the world's applause are Right and Justice … Envy is the great leveller: if it cannot level things up, it will level them down; and the words constantly in its mouth are 'My Rights' and 'My Wrongs.' At its best, Envy is a climber and a snob; at its worst, it is a destroyer … Whereas Avarice is the sin of the Haves against the Have-Nots, Envy is the sin of the Have-Nots against the Haves.[14]

As a destroyer, Envy has been responsible for undermining the foundations of society. It is responsible for character assassination, for the debunking of religion and for other manifestations of postmodern iconoclasm:

Courage was debunked, patriotism was debunked, learning and art were debunked, love was debunked, and with it family affection and the virtues of obedience, veneration and solidarity. Age was debunked by youth and youth by age. Psychologists stripped bare the pretensions of reason and conscience and self-control, saying that these were only the respectable disguises of unmentionable unconscious impulses. Honour was debunked with peculiar virulence, and good faith, and unselfishness...[15]

In politics, Envy manifests itself in the clamour for rights and the denigration of duty. In the field of morals, it derides virtue to such an extent that anything which others venerate is always its enemy: 'Envy cannot bear to admire or respect; it cannot bear to be grateful.'[16]

The sixth deadly sin, that of Sloth, was described with evocative power by Sayers and quoted with evident relish by Schumacher:

In the world it calls itself Tolerance; but in hell it is called Despair. It is the accomplice of the other sins and their worst punishment. It is the sin which believes in nothing, cares for nothing, seeks to know nothing, interferes with nothing, enjoys nothing, loves nothing, hates nothing, finds purpose in nothing, lives for nothing, and only remains alive because there is nothing it would die for. We have known it far too well for many years. The only thing perhaps that we have not known about it is that it is a mortal sin.[17]

Sayers affirmed that the other sins provided a cloak for Sloth. Gluttony with its 'whirl of dancing, dining, sports'; Avarice with its materialistic diversions; Envy with its gossip and scandal; Wrath with its loud complaints about the faults of others; Lust with its 'round of dreary promiscuity that passes for bodily vigour'; all are disguises for 'the empty heart and the empty brain and the empty soul' of Sloth.[18] Yet even Sloth was not the deadliest of the deadly sins:

> But the head and origin of all sin is the basic sin of Superbia or Pride ... It is the sin of trying to be as God. It is the sin which proclaims that Man can produce out of his own wits, and his own impulses and his own imagination the standards by which he lives: that Man is fitted to be his own judge. It is Pride which turns man's virtues into deadly sins ... The name under which Pride walks the world at this moment is the Perfectibility of Man, or the doctrine of Progress; and its speciality is the making of blueprints for Utopia and establishing the Kingdom of Man on earth.[19]

Self-centred

By placing humanity, or the Self, instead of God at the centre of gravity, the sin of Pride 'throws the whole structure of things into the ruin called Judgement'.[20]

The extent to which the materialist ethos is at loggerheads with Christianity and the other world faiths can be gauged by comparing its attitude to these sins. Lust, envy, avarice, gluttony and pride are all employed as key marketing tools. Instead of being sins to avoid they have become pleasures to indulge. Lust is 'sex appeal'; envy is 'keeping up with the Joneses'; avarice is 'being successful or upwardly mobile'; gluttony is always wanting more; and pride is the essential selfishness that makes all the others seem desirable. The seven deadly sins of Christianity have become the seven deadly virtues of consumerism.

The effect of this consumerist religion on its disciples is readily discernible from recent surveys. Between 1967 and 1990, the share of students entering college in the United States who believed it essential to be 'very well off financially' rose from 44 to 74 per cent. The share who believed it essential to develop a meaningful philosophy of life dropped from 83 to 43 per cent. Similarly, high school seniors in the US, polled from 1976 to 1990, displayed waning interest in 'finding purpose and meaning in life' compared with an increasing appetite for the artefacts of consumer society. The proportion ranking 'having lots of money' as 'extremely important' rose from less than half in 1977 to almost two-thirds in 1986, making it top priority in the list of life goals. In Japan the Institute of Statistical Mathematics has asked Japanese citizens to select the philosophy that most closely approximates their own. Between 1953 and the mid-1980s the share selecting to 'live a pure and just life' declined from 29 per cent to 9 per cent, while the share opting to 'live a life that suits your own taste' rose from 21 per cent to 38 per cent.[21] It is little wonder that the Disneyland near Tokyo attracts almost as many visitors as Mecca or the Vatican.

Again, this new religion is not really new at all. Twenty-three centuries ago Aristotle observed that 'the avarice of mankind is insatiable' because as soon as a desire is satisfied a new desire takes its place. 'So the wearing of wild beasts' skins has gone out of fashion,' wrote the Roman philosopher Lucretius a century before Christ. 'Skins yesterday, purple and gold today – such are the baubles that embitter human life with resentment.'[22]

Unchanging Truths

The more things change, the more they remain the same. Only the facts of life have changed, whereas the truths of life are unchanging. The same old problems – greed, envy, pride, etc. – require the same old solutions. 'In fact,' wrote Schumacher, 'there is a marvellously subtle and realistic teaching available in the doctrines of the Four Cardinal Virtues, which is completely relevant and appropriate to the modern predicament.'[23] He continues:

> *The Latin names of the four cardinal virtues* – prudentia, justitia, fortitudo *and* temperantia – *denote rather higher orders of human excellence than their English derivatives – prudence, justice, fortitude and temperance. We can see at once that* temperantia, *that is, the virtue of self-control, discipline, and moderation, which preserves and defends order in the individual and in the environment – we can see that this is the virtue most needed and at the same time most conspicuous by its absence in the modern world. Our obsession with so-called material progress … recognizes no bounds and is thus the clearest possible demonstration of* intemperantia.

Pre-empting possible objections to the discussion of such ancient Christian teachings when we could be talking practically about environmental problems, Schumacher posed the following question: 'Yet, as the real cause of our troubles is *intemperantia*, how could we hope to bring pollution or population or the consumption of resources under control, if we cannot control ourselves and are not prepared to study the question of self-control?'

Moving to the virtue of *prudentia* – prudence – Schumacher described it as 'a clear-eyed, magnanimous recognition of reality'. This was a moral achievement which required that all selfish interests be silenced. 'Only out of the stillness of this silence can spring perception in accordance with reality.'

Prudence was as relevant to our present predicament as temperance because it involved our relationship with nature. 'The old Christian teaching maintains that nothing blinds the individual and destroys prudence so effectively as greed and envy.'

In discussing the virtue of justice, Schumacher quoted St Thomas Aquinas, who said that justice not only orders man in himself but also the life of men together. Meanwhile the function of the cardinal virtue of fortitude was to fight, by endurance as well as by attack, the evil power of greed and envy. 'Easy-going optimism that "science will solve all problems" or that we can somehow achieve a social-political system so perfect that no one has to be good, is the most current form of cowardice.'

Schumacher concluded by insisting that virtue was not an optional extra in the desire to change the world, it was absolutely essential. The cardinal virtues were of cardinal importance:

It is because our social system not merely neglects but actively discourages the cardinal virtues of prudence, justice, fortitude and temperantia, that we are in trouble with the environment. Not surprisingly, therefore, many people clamour for a different social system ... But it must be emphasized that just as the social system shapes the environment, so our basic philosophy shapes our social system. Unless this philosophy changes, the system cannot change in its essential nature – however much it may change in terms of the distribution of power and wealth, or in terms of structure or administrative method ...

Let us face it: it is easy to ask for 'new values' without specifying what they are and how they are to be attained. The realization of value is impossible without the practice of virtue.

Life-Giving Virtues

To conclude, we will offer as an antidote to the seven deadly sins of consumerism, Seven Life-Giving Virtues which could help to save the planet from humanity, and humanity from itself. Collectively they represent what Schumacher called a way of making visible a viable future.

First is non-violence. We must learn to live in harmony with each other and with nature. To do otherwise is to harm ourselves and our environment. Either the gentle shall inherit the earth or else nobody will.

Second is smallness. Humans are human-sized and need a human-sized future. We need to live in such a way that the *wholeness* of our nature – soul and body and spirit – can flourish.

Third is satisfaction. We need to remember that to be satisfied is to have enough, not more then enough. We need to temper our selfish desires through self-sacrifice and self-limitation.

Fourth is humility. Without a sense of our own smallness, through humility, we will be subject to the sin of pride, which is at the heart of human greed and self-centredness. As individuals we are important, but not all-important.

Fifth is co-operation. We must work with each other, not against each other, in pursuit of a lasting justice and a sustainable future.

Sixth is good husbandry. We must never forget that our natural environment has its own laws of sustainability which we override at our peril. Organic farming and appropriate technology, which works with nature and not against it, are the only way forward.

Seventh is putting ends before means. As Schumacher never tired of telling us, we must always work out our practical realities from the higher realities, not vice versa.

These seven practical steps towards a sustainable future are only possible if they are built on the sure foundations of the four cardinal virtues. If we begin now to live virtuously, we can start to put our principles into practice. For those who accept the ancient wisdom in its entirety, these principles may be seven steps to heaven. Either way, even if they don't bring heaven on earth, they will at least bring heaven a little closer to earth.

The final words belong to Schumacher:

> *The violence that is in the process of destroying the world is the cold, calculating, detached, heartless, and relentless violence that springs from over-extended minds working out of control of under-developed hearts. A person who does not feel his thoughts but merely entertains them ... is capable of limitless violence ... He is supremely rational; for him, the only certainty is his own death, and ... his own death is equivalent to the disappearance of the world. He stands at the pinnacle of ego-centricity and potential violence. Pure reason can worship only itself, and only the heart can conceive the idea of sacrifice.*
>
> *Modern civilization can survive only if it begins again to educate the heart ... for modern human beings are now far too clever to be able to survive without wisdom.*[24]

1 Dorothy L. Sayers, *Begin Here*, London: Victor Gollancz, 1940, p. 152.

2 *Resurgence*, Vol. 7, No. 3, July–August 1976.

3 Ibid.

4 *Resurgence*, Vol. 5, No. 5, November–December 1974.

5 *Resurgence*, Vol. 7, No. 3.

6 Ibid.

7 Ibid.

8 Ibid.

9 *Resurgence*, Vol. 5, No. 5.

10 Ibid.

11 E.F. Schumacher, *A Guide for the Perplexed*, London: Abacus, 1977, p. 157.

12 Ibid., p. 158.

13 Dorothy L. Sayers, *The Other Six Deadly Sins*, London: Methuen, fifth edn., 1944, pp. 11–13.

14 Ibid., pp. 19–20.

15 Ibid., p. 22.

16 Ibid.

17 Ibid., pp. 23–4.

18 Ibid., p. 25.

19 Ibid., p. 26.

20 Ibid., p. 27.

21 Alan Thein Durning, *How Much Is Enough? The Consumer Society and the Future of the Earth*, New York: W.W. Norton and Company, 1992, p. 34.

22 Ibid., p. 37.

23 *Resurgence*, Vol. 5, No. 5.

24 *Resurgence*, Vol. 7, No. 6, January–February 1977.

Index